The Embodied Core

A Woman's Guide to Easing Back and Pelvic Pain, Naturally

Jill Robinson

Organic Pilates & Holistic Health

ISBN: 978-173945250-6

Contents

Welcome to The Embodied Core

The Complete Guide to Easing Your Back and Pelvic Pain, and Embodying Your Core Naturally

"Embodiment, for me, means that you can listen to your body, know what it needs, and act upon those needs."

Are you feeling her, the old lady creeping in? Your joints becoming more painful, you creak when you get out of your chair, or maybe you're just feeling like you don't have the energy anymore to do the things you love?

I hear you, and I've heard this from countless women I've helped over the years. They're worn out, tired, in pain, and they're realising they need to start taking action to stop the general decline into old age.

That's the thing: it creeps up on you. Before you know it, you've put on ten pounds, your clothes don't fit, it hurts to move, and your energy levels have slumped to an all-time low.

It's hard to know where to start. Can you do anything about it?

Welcome, and yes, you can make a start, and I'm here to tell you it doesn't have to be difficult either. In fact, throughout this book, I'm going to positively encourage you to just make small tweaks to your lifestyle. No bone crunching workouts that last for hours, no rubbish diets that only allow you to eat kale and cabbage soup, and you don't have to stop doing the things you love. I'm going to be encouraging you to eat a beautiful rainbow of nutritious meals, show you how and what movements you can do whilst fitting them into your busy life, and get you back in touch with yourself.

You know that version of you who was living her best life, until life, kids, and hormones threw a few curveballs your way? Well, she's still inside of you. We just have to do a bit of digging, planting and pruning to get her back out and facing the world.

This is a journey into your soul. We can go as deep as you want with it. Learning how to heal your back and pelvic pain will require a lot of soul searching; we are not just a physical body, we're a mental, emotional, and spiritual body. All four bodies are of equal importance.

We need to give ourselves space and time, to reconnect and to ultimately heal. Space and time, two magical words, no quick fixes here, just sound, solid advice that I know works.

One of my mentors, Paul Chek, always says, *"Men are like dump trucks, and women are Ferraris."*

Men's back pain can usually be fixed through mechanical means, through correct movements and strengthening their muscles around the spinal structures. However, various factors often make women's back pain more complex. Women require much more finesse.

In this book, I have collected all the information and research I have undertaken while working with women. I have also included the latest scientific findings on women's back and pelvic pain. It is noteworthy that researchers have only recently begun to explore gender differences in women's back and pelvic pain, and this growing body of research is very much welcomed. However, there is still much more to learn.

To complement this book, I have prepared a 6-week programme in written and video format. You can access it by scanning the QR code (on page 145) and providing your email address. Once you do that, you'll receive a weekly email from me for the next six weeks with videos of all the techniques I mention in the book. Reading about the research and exercises is useful, but you must do the work. It all starts from the inside out.

Starting to heal yourself may seem overwhelming, particularly after experiencing years of pain. But it is possible. Working alongside your current medical advice, taking small steps such as doing a few daily movements, and developing consistent healthy habits can lead you towards progress.

This book might introduce you to new and thought-provoking ideas you haven't encountered before. Take the ones that resonate and let the others bed in. You never know what might seed in the future—that's how we evolve and grow. Your body possesses profound wisdom and holds the answers you seek. It surpasses both of us in its intelligence. Paying attention to your body lets you know what needs to be done and when. I'm a big believer in cosmic timing: when the student is ready the teacher will appear.

This book will aid you on your path to recovery and becoming the best version of you, ready to face the future with a positive outlook and confidence in your body. Feeling and looking amazing is not something that is reserved for the young—you're about to enter your prime!

The techniques contained within have proven

beneficial to my clients over the years and will be equally beneficial to you.

How To Use This Book

Initially, this book started out as a mini guide, but it's grown as I realised women need to know this stuff. There's nothing in this book that I don't practice myself—all the practices and advice I feel are important. Often, women ask me, "Why have I never been taught this before?" I wanted to include everything to get you started on a healthy path. Within all these topics I could go much deeper, but we need to start somewhere, and I didn't want to overwhelm you.

To begin, it's good to establish where you are currently regarding your physical and emotional state. Get yourself a beautiful journal and start answering a few of the questions at the back of this book. Be honest, there's only you going to see them.

Be open-minded and trust the process. From small acorns, mighty oak trees grow.

This book covers various techniques and practices that you may find helpful. Start with the easy ones for you. For the others, I recommend that you create a plan and determine when and how to integrate them. My approach emphasises consistency, aiming for small but frequent improvements. To successfully develop new habits, you should begin with one and maintain it for a few weeks until it becomes a natural part of your routine. Taking on lots of new habits simultaneously is never a good thing—you'll be setting yourself up to fail.

You will find many of the top tips are repeated or are similar in each of the sections—that's because THEY WORK. I will continue to bang the drum for them.

The beginning of this book is mostly the physical and the scientific; the second half of the book is mostly the spiritual and esoteric. Both are of equal value. You may find that you resonate more with one than the other—that's fine, but know that we need to be both Yin and Yang. Being healthy is all about balance, not just the physical, but your thoughts, words, actions, and deeds.

It's important to be patient and show your body some love. With time, you'll feel a stronger connection to your core and become more embodied. Embodiment, for me, means that you can listen to your body, know what it needs, and act upon those needs. Once you learn to listen, you'll be moving and grooving without pain or discomfort.

Remember that girl who thought she could take on the world? The one who was confident, felt amazing, and had no fear? Well, she's still there, and we're going to bring her back—but a wiser and even more beautiful version.

Make sure you scan the QR Code (on page 145) and enter your best email address and I'll send you the six-week program via email. I promise there'll be no spam.

Are you ready to make a start? Well, let's begin at the very beginning.

Who is Your Guide?

"You cannot live your best life if you feel like crap."

Hello, I'm Jill and I've written this book because I've spent years studying and teaching women of all ages, with all sorts of conditions and injuries. There are a few things I've learned over that time, and this book is very much a bridge between the scientific and the spiritual. Over my years of practice, I've come to realise that the spiritual is the most important of the four bodies of wellness (physical, mental, emotional, and spiritual) because it's the one that drives the others. Ultimately dis-ease begins in the psyche way before it manifests in the body (unless you have an accident), so a lot of the practices I detail at the end of this book are the more spiritual ones that you can begin to incorporate straight away.

I've just entered my 50s and I've spent all of my 40s learning as much as I could about physical training, hormones, nutrition, anatomy, and physiology. It was an entirely selfish endeavour, as I wanted to prepare myself as much as I could for menopause. Along the way, I've put into practice what works for me, and I'm now the fittest and healthiest I've ever been. I believe we all have the right to feel this way, but we need the space and time to reconnect. I've completely connected to my core, full embodiment body, mind and soul.

I specialise in movement, Pilates, women's strength training, holistic lifestyle coaching, Breathwork Facilitator and teacher, women's circles, podcasting, writing, aromatherapist, crystal healer, and an ecstatic dance DJ. Phew, that's quite a list!

Moreover, I'm a wife, mother of teenagers, mother of Labradors, business owner, and passionate about health and wellness.

I've been teaching fitness for over 25 years. I now run a popular Pilates studio in County Durham. My mission is to help women and men become fitter, stronger, and healthier. Everyone can heal their own body, and our bodies possess an innate wisdom that can provide all the answers we need if we only listen.

I always say, "You cannot live your best life if you feel like crap!"

I've worked with countless women, all doing their best for everyone, but often that means sacrificing themselves. You cannot give what you do not have; eventually, that will catch up. Something's got to give, and usually that's your physical, mental, spiritual, and emotional health.

Your body is constantly sending you signals; are you listening? Every single cell in your body is listening to what you tell it, so make sure you're saying good things.

Movement is medicine. I know this to be true.

I believe in fusing cutting-edge science with ancient wisdom. That's where the alchemy lies. Dismissing remedies used for centuries because science has not yet acknowledged them is crazy. Drawing from my experiences with real women, I understand what methods are effective and how to introduce them gently. I draw deeply not only on physical but on spiritual practices too—I've been able to read Tarot cards since I was 10 years old; my spiritual practices have been running longer than my physical ones. I don't believe you can separate the two. I'm just as happy banging my drum in the woods, as I am swinging my kettlebell in the gym.

When you start becoming more embodied and connected to your core, you will feel your energy levels rising. I firmly believe that by elevating your energy levels, you can cultivate healthy habits and make the necessary changes for a more fulfilling life. Raising your vibration by being mindful of your thoughts, words, and actions can help you improve your mindset and promote healing.

The Dalai Lama once said, "The World will be saved by the Western Woman." I'd like to change this slightly and say, "The World will be changed by the rested Western Woman"! The stressed out, all giving, sacrificing, and in-pain western woman is in no state to change the world. We owe it not just to us, but to the world to be free from pain and living our best lives fully embodied and in tune with ourselves and the planet.

Are you ready to make a start reconnecting your core and embodying your life? When healing any injury, you may uncover more about yourself than you realise.

> *"Neo, sooner or later you're going to realise, just as I did, that there's a difference between knowing the path and walking the path."*—Morpheus (*The Matrix*)

Are you ready to start walking the path to a pain-free life? Let's do this!

Jill x

Chapter 1

What Does It Mean To You To Live Your Best Life?

I don't ask this question flippantly. What would you do if money and time were not an issue? What job or career path would you do if you could make your choices again? Are you yearning for something different?

When we start to step into our "Crone" Archetype or Wise Woman energy (see page 106), we begin to see life differently. We begin to question our choices and our life path. There's a reason why most marriages fail for couples in their 50s: the women are waking up to the question "is this it?"

The Crone teaches us we have a choice, we women are powerful beings, and it's only until we reach this level of maturity that we start to understand just how powerful we are. Historically, the world has silenced us, tortured us for speaking out, and made us feel like second-class citizens. Who burned witches at the stake? Men, that's who—because they were scared of the feminine power. We've had to hide our true selves, live under the patriarchal system of "just keep going," work harder and faster, show no weakness.

When we step into our Crone or Wise Woman Energy, we start seeing our beautiful planet that's being destroyed, the ways of working that advantage men, that our bodies are going through changes—it makes us mad. Mid-life women are angry.

We need to channel that fire into making ourselves the best version, before old age creeps in.

It's never too late to make a start.

Embodiment Practices

Have you ever found yourself saying "yes" to something but feeling like your entire body is screaming "no", or vice versa?

In this book, I often mention the concept of "being embodied" but what exactly does that mean? And what exactly is "embodying your core"?

Achieving embodiment is a process that takes years of practice and requires ongoing effort. When we respond to a question or someone's touch, we do so in our minds, but our bodies may feel differently. For example, perhaps when you were a child you had an uncle you were always forced to kiss goodbye, but it never felt right. Or maybe you feel you should be grateful for something, but your body is telling you otherwise.

Practising embodiment, we tune into our body's signals and use them to make decisions rather than relying solely on our brain or societal pressures. It's essential to ensure that our entire body is on board with a decision rather than just our minds.

To fully reconnect with our bodies, we need to access our whole body, including our core, which bridges our upper and lower bodies. We tend to feel emotions and sensations in our gut, so that connection can be disrupted when we experience an injury or trauma. By using full-body methods, we can restore that connection and become more attuned to our bodies, get back in touch with our gut feeling.

Embodiment practices are closely linked to our Central Nervous System (CNS), responsible for our fight-or-flight response. We can incorporate embodied practices into our healing journey by asking ourselves questions about what triggers our CNS response and who or what is present in those situations.

We need to keep tuning in to ourselves, into our spine, into our core. What does it need right now? How can I make myself feel better? What does my body need? Keep bringing our awareness back into ourselves. It takes practise but the more we do it, the more we begin to notice the signals when they're tiny, rather than when they start screaming at us.

Women are Different to Men—No Sh*t, Sherlock!

It is estimated that 80% of people will have Lower Back Pain (LBP) at some point in their lives, with a higher percentage being women. LBP is the primary cause of disability in adults of all ages, with the World Health Organisation confirming that musculoskeletal co-morbidities are the most debilitating conditions.

Until recently, medical trials have excluded women, which is a concerning 50% of the population. Shrinking conventional treatments designed for men to fit women's needs has proven ineffective and is unlikely to work, ever.

According to a study conducted by Bento et al. in Brazil in 2020, they observed the causes of back pain in men and women. The study revealed that 60.9% of women suffer from LBP compared to 39.1% of men.

Research has shown that women are more prone to experiencing lower back pain (LBP) due to factors related to their work environment and ergonomics compared to men. This could be attributed to the nature of women's roles at work, which may involve more computer or desk-based work and differences in how they perform tasks and cope with stress.

The statement's authors have unintentionally discovered the actual reason behind women experiencing more back pain than men, as they mention in their report:

"In addition, because women generally have more responsibility at home and work and spend more time performing household tasks than men, they are more likely to be exposed to some risk factors such as inadequate static posture."

You don't say!

In summary, women at work often have different roles and responsibilities than men and have more household tasks. As a result, women experience stress differently. The causes of back pain in women often differ from those in men. I'm certain women have long been aware of this! And they wonder why we suffer from stress differently.

The drivers for women with back pain are very different from that for men.

Back pain in women differs from that in men, and recent research findings reveal that the usual drivers of smoking, obesity, and a sedentary lifestyle may not be as significant for women as they are for men. These differences have been previously overlooked.

According to a study by Smith et al. in 2013, there is a strong link between Chronic Back Pain (CBP) in women and Stress Urinary Incontinence (which is the involuntary loss of urine when coughing, sneezing, or laughing, like when jumping on a trampoline). The study suggests that training the pelvic floor muscles can effectively manage CBP.

Another excellent study of over 38,000 women by Smith & Hodges in 2006 found:

"When incontinence and breathing difficulties were considered, obesity and physical activity were not consistently associated with back pain. In contrast, ratios for often having back pain were higher for women with incontinence than those without. Similarly, mid-aged and older women had higher odds of having back pain often when they experienced breathing difficulties compared to women with no breathing problems. Unlike obesity and physical activity, disorders of continence and respiration were strongly related to frequent back pain."

Err, say what? Breathing problems and continence issues are more commonly linked to back pain in women than obesity or a sedentary lifestyle? If your doctor blames your back pain on being overweight or inactive next time you visit, you can share this information with them.

So, bladder and breathing play a more significant role in back pain than previously considered. Let us look at another B—the bowels!

In another study by Smith & Hodges in 2008, they found gastrointestinal issues are a strong indicator of back pain:

"Possible factors that may account for this relationship include referred pain through viscerosomatic convergence, altered pain perception, increased spinal loading when straining during defecation, or reduced support of the abdominal contents and spine secondary to changes in the function of the abdominal muscles."

Simply put, when you strain to use the loo, it puts

pressure on your spine. This can add unnecessary stress to your spine and contribute to your body's overall pain volume. (Refer to Chapter 2 for more information.)

So, we have learned the following:

- Breathing Correctly
- Bladder Health
- Bowel Health

Research has shown that factors such as posture, daily activities, and reproductive health play a more significant role in causing back and pelvic pain in women than previously believed. This differs from the standard advice of exercising more, eating less, or relying on painkillers.

Also, stress and work can play a significant role (maybe, the two are linked for you).

THERE ARE THINGS YOU CAN DO TO HELP YOUR BACK PAIN

And we're going to make a start with the three things on the list. Are you ready to start making some changes to reconnect your core?

Chapter 2

Pain-Free Living—Can It Be Done?

Taking charge of your pain means taking control of your body. You can significantly improve your pain levels by using full-body techniques and integrated movements that work all your muscles. This may require some time and effort, but achieving it is possible. Remember, it's not just about targeting the tight or in-pain muscles but using techniques that engage your entire body.

Embodying your core will require time and effort, and there is no quick fix. It's a process that requires endurance and patience.

We can begin by understanding the nature of pain.

What is Pain?

In July 2020, the ISAP (International Association for the Study of Pain) revised its definition of pain for the first time in over 40 years. The current definition is:

"An unpleasant sensory and emotional experience associated with or resembling that associated with actual or potential tissue damage" and is expanded upon by adding six key notes and the etymology of the word pain for further valuable context.

These five notes are (in my words, to translate the medical terminology):

1. Pain is individual: your thoughts, beliefs, upbringing, and education influence your pain levels.
2. Pain does not always infer tissue damage. Indeed, the tissues can be long healed, but the pain remains.
3. We learn concepts of pain through our life experiences.
4. A person's report of an experience in pain should be respected.
5. Although pain is there to help us and protect us, it can affect our ability to function.

Interesting, eh? Let's take the first part of the definition — "...resembling that associated with actual or potential tissue damage."

Is it possible to feel pain even if there's no actual tissue damage? Yes, it is. Sometimes your brain sends pain signals to protect you from potential harm. While the existing body tissue can usually repair itself in three to six months, the pain in the affected area can persist for years. This doesn't mean the pain is imaginary or "in your head", but rather it's the brain's way of alerting you to potential danger.

Pain is your body's way of protecting you, your life experiences, your ability to cope with stress, and your social status; all of these play a vital role in the volume of your pain and your ability to turn that volume up or down. Pain is not a single cause, but some strategies will help integrate using your whole body for pain management.

How to Manage Pain?

Lorimer Moseley and David Butler devised and described a method called DIMs (Dangers in Me) and SIMs (Safety in Me) in their book Explain Pain. The idea is to identify any triggers that would ramp up your pain volume or turn it down (I would say this is the same as embodiment practices, but worded scientifically).

After much research, they found that pain is primarily constructed in the brain; it's individual and can be changed. They devised a specialist tool called the "Protectometer", an imaginary tool with danger on one side and safety on the other. When the body goes into "danger" mode, it can present itself as spasms, fatigue, pain, anxiety etc. They concluded that you would have pain when your brain perceives that there is more "danger in me" than "safety in me."

The idea is to create a list of DIMs, so when your brain perceives there might be trouble ahead and a list of SIMs, there are things you can do to calm and reassure your brain. They originate from the same list.

Things to think about:

- What you see, hear, smell, taste, and touch.
- Things you do.
- Things you say.
- Something you think and believe.
- Places you go.
- People in your life.
- Things happening in your body.

An example of a DIM is if I drive down a road where I had an accident and feel pain in my neck. An example of a SIM would be when I feel the sun on my face, I feel calm and happy, and it reminds me of being on holiday.

Let's begin and list all the DIMs and SIMs in your life. Grab a cup of tea, take a few deep breaths, and start on your list.

When you've written your list, how did it make you feel? Did you have more DIMs than SIMs? Can you reduce your DIMs and increase your SIMs?

The idea is to overwhelm the DIMs with SIMs. Your body tells your brain when to ramp up the pain. Let us see if we can keep sending our body good signals to keep the pain volume down.

Other ways to manage pain include Breathwork (see Breathing Section) and movement; the days of bed rest for back pain are long gone.

Pain as a Teacher

Experiencing pain, whether physical or emotional, can offer valuable lessons, although it might not feel like it at the time. Pain can bring awareness to areas of our physical, mental, or emotional health that require attention. It can serve as a wake-up call, prompting us to become more self-aware and attuned to our needs and limitations. I know from working with individuals who have experienced pain, they are more motivated and determined to do the work.

I spent a year with Plantar Fasciitis; it was so painful, I could hardly walk. I now do my foot strengthening exercises every day without fail. I'm never going back to that pain. Every day I send love into my feet and tune into them to make sure they're happy feet!

When you've experienced pain, you become more

empathic and compassionate towards others going through similar struggles. Some of the best teachers I know have personally overcome serious injuries or conditions. Your pain can become your power.

Pain can push you out of your comfort zone and lead to personal breakthroughs and self-discovery. You might never have been motivated to pick up this book if you'd not been in pain. You also savour the moments when you're not in pain. It makes you live in the moment and appreciate your health.

Can you think of anything else pain has taught you?

At the back of this book is a list of questions you can begin to reflect on in your journal about what your pain is teaching you.

Chapter 3

Manage Your Stress

Stress is THE most common issue I have observed working with women over the years. It seems unreasonable to expect women to work 40-hour weeks, raise families, maintain a tidy home, and still look youthful and attractive (while forbidden to age). Plus, women must deal with the challenges of perimenopause, hot flushes, unpredictable hormones, mood swings, sleepless nights, weight gain, teenagers, and generally feeling like crap.

As a society, we should reconsider the workload expectations for women. While we strive for equality, we must recognise men and women are different. We shouldn't expect women to be the same as men in order to be considered equal. Comparing them is like comparing fire and water—both are equally good at what they do but serve different purposes.

Anyway, let me get back on track. Women are stressed!

Here are some important facts to keep in mind about stress:

- Whether the stress is real or perceived, your body will respond in the same way.
- The upper trapezius muscles in your neck and your pelvic floor muscles are the first to react to stress.
- Factors beyond just external events can cause stress. Not eating the right foods, drinking alcohol, smoking, lack of physical activity, and exposure to chemicals are all known to trigger stress.

It's hard to avoid stress in today's world. Our devices and the constant stream of information they provide can be overwhelming. We live in a fast-paced society where there's always something we need to do or have, and our to-do lists seem never-ending.

Our bodies were designed for a different time, not the present day. Evolution has yet to catch up with the rapid changes of the past 50 years alone. Our predecessors lived in small communities with about 30 individuals, which is a far cry from today's vast global social media networks, where thousands can scrutinise our every move.

Your body's stress response is thus:

When your brain perceives a potential threat (whether the stress is real or perceived), the hypothalamus sends a signal to your central nervous system (CNS). This prompts an alert, triggering the release of stress hormones, such as adrenaline and cortisol.

The stress response has two branches—the para-sympathetic response (PNS—rest and digest) and the sympathetic (SNS—fight or flight) response.

When you experience stress and the SNS is activated, the two hormones cortisol and adrenaline are released. They increase your heart rate, redirect blood flow from organs to muscles and heart, and suppress your immune and digestive systems. Stress can also lower sex drive; no babies are getting made if the body is under stress. However, once the stressor is gone, your body should return to a state of balance known as homeostasis.

But what if the stressor does not go away?

What if it's something you're purposely doing to yourself, like drinking alcohol?

Think about how the stress is contributing to your pain volume.

Many times, we unintentionally subject our bodies to stress without realising it. For instance, when we don't consume enough nutrients, the body will not only crave more food, it will also trigger an SNS response. This means cortisol and adrenaline will be present in our system consistently. If these hormones remain in our bodies for an extended period, it can lead to various issues.

These stress hormones are classified as "catabolic" hormones and can negatively affect our immune system, joints, and muscles.

Chadi G Abdallah and Paul Geha's 2017 research paper suggests stress and chronic pain share similar mechanisms. They activate the same brain areas and are two sides of the same coin. Although stress and pain responses are natural ways to keep us safe, their chronic nature can lead to issues.

Both stress and pain serve a purpose, but when they're both present, they can intensify each other. By managing our stress levels, we can reduce the volume of our pain.

Becoming both connected to your core, and an embodied person, means becoming deeply aware of our nervous system reactions and how that influences pain and stress. You become aware when your SNS response is activated: you will feel it in your body. The more embodied you become, the more you'll sense the little signals, so you'll be able to do something about it before you have a full-blown stress response. Activating the PNS response is something we can do consciously. I'll talk about this later in the book, but just for now, know that you can take control of both the SNS and PNS responses.

Start to notice what makes you react and how you bring yourself back. Notice how your pain and stress response are intertwined with each other.

Your cycle of stress may look like the one below. Does it sound familiar?

THE CYCLE OF STRESS

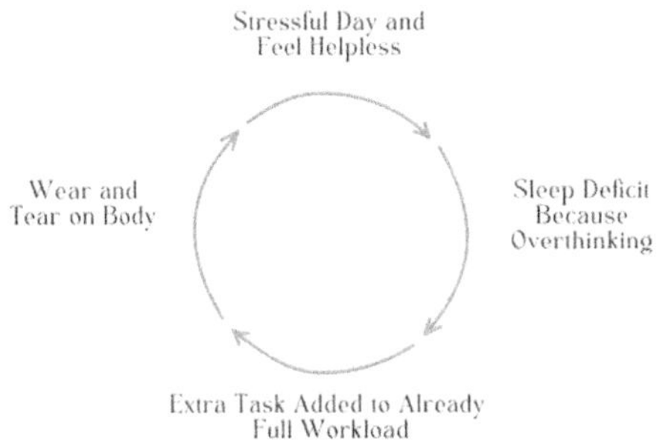

Stress occurs when we feel that we lack the resources to meet our demands.

Chapter 4

Why Anatomy Matters

As someone passionate about anatomy, a clear understanding of your body's structures can aid in visualising your pain and the surrounding areas. This knowledge can also help you make informed decisions about movements and communicating your experiences more effectively.

Understanding your body's anatomy is crucial to better identifying the root cause of your pain. Knowing about different structures like bones, muscles, tendons, ligaments, and nerves can assist you in accurately pinpointing the exact area of discomfort. I recommend researching the anatomy of the spine to help you identify the specific area that's causing you pain.

When you talk to healthcare professionals about your pain, it's helpful to have a basic understanding of anatomy to describe your symptoms accurately. This will allow you to communicate your pain's location, type, and intensity, which will help doctors or therapists make a more precise diagnosis and create an effective treatment plan.

Knowing the anatomy of the affected area can aid in

understanding the available treatment options. For instance, if you experience back pain, comprehending the structure of the spine and the surrounding muscles can help you grasp why particular exercises, medications, or therapies are suggested.

Developing knowledge of anatomy can help prevent pain and encourage self-care. It enables you to recognise possible causes or triggers for discomfort and make informed choices about your lifestyle, exercise routines, and ergonomics to prevent or alleviate pain.

When I talk about the anatomy of the spine to my clients, they often have lightbulb moments. You don't need to be a doctor or have a PhD to understand anatomy. A doctor once told me that being knowledgeable about your condition can be helpful for them to make decisions.

The key is to take small steps towards regaining control of your health instead of being overwhelmed by diagnoses and treatments. Start by taking notes of your symptoms, identifying triggers, and understanding your anatomy—this is how you can become more self-sufficient.

Anatomy of the Spine In Brief

Most people associate back pain with the lower back, but the spine runs from the coccyx in your butt up to the atlas bone in the skull. Pain can occur anywhere along the spine, including the neck, shoulders, and pelvis.

Technically, your spine has five sections.

1. Cervical—your neck bones, the minor vertebrae.
2. Thoracic—the mid-section, where your rib bones attach.

3. Lumbar—the largest vertebrae that provide all the stability and support.
4. Sacrum—four fused vertebrae at the bottom of the spine that form part of the pelvic girdle.
5. Coccyx—a small, slightly moveable bone right at the base of the spine that holds the attachments for the pelvic floor muscles.

The human spine has 33 bones that form a super strong structure enabling movement and standing upright. The spine has a natural S-shape that acts as a shock absorber and maintains balance while in motion.

The spine has intervertebral discs between each vertebra that function as shock absorbers and prevent bones from rubbing against each other. These discs resemble car tyres and lose their natural plumpness and elasticity as we age, leading to problems.

Muscles of the Spine

The spine is supported by two primary muscle groups: flexors and extensors. The extensor muscles are at the back of the body and maintain an upright posture, preventing collapse. Flexors are at the front of the body and include the abdominal wall muscles, which facilitate forward bending. Additionally, lateral muscles need to be incorporated into a comprehensive strength-training program to develop a strong "core".

Did you know your spine is incredibly strong? In fact, under tests, the ligaments in your lumbar spine are stronger than steel wire. Sometimes, people are afraid to move because they worry about "breaking their backs"—but unless you experience a severe accident, it's highly unlikely your back will break. Understanding the structure of your spine can help you realise just how strong and stable it is. You can increase your strength and stability by mobilising and strengthening the muscles and structures surrounding your spine. It's essential to keep moving and avoid staying still for too long, as this can cause your spine to become stiff and dehydrated.

Incorporating regular, quality movement into your routine can benefit your spine health and mental and emotional well-being. If you suffer from chronic back pain, beginning an exercise program may seem daunting, but starting with gentle movements and deep breathing each day can gradually improve your condition. Although there may be days when the pain returns, they will become less frequent as you experience more good days.

A Healthy Spine Needs Good Nutrition

"If we could give every individual the right amount of nourishment and exercise, not too little and not too much, we would have the safest way to health."—Hippocrates

To maintain a healthy spine and body, it is essential to provide it with the necessary nutrients. More than proper mechanical care is required, as the spine requires the right fuel to support it.

A healthy diet can play a significant role and is often overlooked in maintaining a healthy spine. Foods and nutrients that specifically support spine health are:

- Foods rich in calcium, such as dairy products, leafy greens, and fortified cereals. They can help strengthen bones and prevent conditions like osteoporosis, leading to spinal fractures.
- Vitamin D is essential for calcium absorption and bone health. Vitamin D-rich foods include

fatty fish, egg yolks, and fortified dairy products. You can also get vitamin D from sunlight exposure.
- Omega-3 fatty acids: found in fatty fish, walnuts, and flaxseeds, omega-3 fatty acids have anti-inflammatory properties that can help reduce spine inflammation.
- Fruits and vegetables are rich in antioxidants, which can help to prevent damage to the spine from free radicals. (Free radicals are unstable atoms that can damage cells and cause inflammation and ageing.)
- Staying hydrated is essential for spinal health, as the discs between the vertebrae are made up of water. Drinking plenty of water can help keep these discs hydrated and functioning properly.

Avoiding foods that can trigger inflammation, like sugary snacks, processed foods, and saturated fats, is crucial to reducing inflammation. For a straightforward approach to diet and nutrition, there's no need to follow a complex diet plan, take excessive supplements, or deprive yourself of food.

Focus on the Just Eat Real Food (JERF) principle.

Chapter 5

Gut Health

The JERF principle is essential in bowel health, too. This is a fascinating and growing area of research. Again, I could write a whole book on this topic, but I will keep it specific to your back and pelvic pain.

The relationship between gut health and back pain is an emerging area of research, and the precise mechanisms still need to be fully understood. However, several potential connections between gut health and back pain are worth exploring.

Research suggests chronic inflammation can affect both gut health and back pain. An imbalance in the gut microbiome and increased intestinal permeability, also known as leaky gut, can lead to poor gut health. This can cause chronic low-grade inflammation that may affect other areas of the body, including the back, leading to discomfort and pain.

The gut and brain are connected through a pathway called the gut-brain axis (also see Polyvagal Theory Section). This pathway allows communication between trillions of microorganisms in the gut (known as the gut microbiome) and the brain. When the gut microbiome is imbalanced, it can affect neurotransmitter production and immune function, influencing pain perception and back pain severity.

Scientists have suggested that disruptions in the gut-brain axis may cause increased sensitivity to pain through "central sensitisation," a condition that makes the central nervous system more sensitive to pain stimuli. This increased sensitivity can contribute to the development or worsening of back pain.

Proper nutrient absorption relies on a healthy gut. A compromised gut can lead to nutrient deficiencies that may affect the health of tissues, muscles, and joints, including those in the back.

The gut produces neurotransmitters and hormones, such as serotonin and gamma-aminobutyric acid (GABA), that regulate mood. Imbalances in these neurotransmitters caused by poor gut health can contribute to stress, anxiety, and depression which, as we've seen, influence pain perception.

Embodying our core requires good gut health. Making a few tweaks to our diet is all it takes.

How to Improve Gut Health

Along with all the lifestyle factors mentioned in this book, there are a few specific to gut health:

1. Eat more fermented foods such as sauerkraut, kombucha, kefir.
2. Use Apple Cider Vinegar (see section below).

3. Include a variety of plants in your diet—I recommend 30 different plants per week (see checklist at the back of the book).
4. Take a pro and pre-biotic.
5. Try not to take antibiotics unless necessary.

Hydration

Staying hydrated is crucial for maintaining good health and can significantly help manage back and pelvic pain in women. Hydration plays a vital role in pain management by keeping the joints, especially those in the back and pelvis, healthy and functioning correctly. The discs between spinal vertebrae comprise a lot of water, allowing them to absorb shocks and remain flexible. When the body is well hydrated, it promotes optimal joint function and lubrication, reducing the likelihood of pain and stiffness.

Dehydration can contribute to the degeneration of spinal discs, leading to back pain. These discs act as cushions between the vertebrae, absorbing pressure and facilitating movement. When dehydrated, the discs may lose some moisture, resulting in reduced cushioning and increased vulnerability to injury or compression of nerves.

Dehydration can lead to muscle cramps, stiffness, and tension, contributing to back and pelvic pain. When dehydrated, muscles may become more prone to spasms and increased sensitivity to pain, like the dreaded cramp.

In women, dehydration can increase the chances of developing urinary tract infections (UTIs), which can cause discomfort, inflammation, and pelvic pain (see chapter on bladder health). To prevent UTIs and associated pain, drink enough water to maintain optimal urinary tract function and flush out bacteria.

How Much Water Should You Drink?

My general rule is around two litres of pure water per day. Herbal teas without milk count towards your water intake.

A good baseline equation, which I learned from Paul Chek, is: your body weight in kg x 0.033 = litres of water to be consumed throughout the day. Thus, a 70kg female would require around 2.3 litres per day.

The key to drinking enough water during the day is to start early—as soon as you get up. I drink half a pint of water with apple cider vinegar every morning first thing. Then that's all I drink all day. Carry a water bottle with you—you'll be surprised how much you can drink if you just keep doing it little and often.

If two litres seem like a lot to you, start with one litre and gradually build up.

A Word on Protein

Did you know eating enough protein can help ease back pain?

Protein promotes muscle growth and repair, strengthening the muscles in your back, and improving your posture. Protein is an essential nutrient that provides the building blocks for muscles and helps repair and maintain tissues in your body. Consuming more protein can support muscle growth and repair, reducing back pain.

Protein can also assist with weight management, as it makes you feel full. Excess weight can strain the back and increase pain.

The amount of protein a woman in her 50s should eat depends on various factors, such as weight, height, physical activity levels, and overall health status. However, as a general guideline, the recommended dietary allowance

(RDA) for protein for women in their 50s is 0.8 grams per kilogram of body weight per day.

For example, if a woman weighs 68 kilograms (150 pounds), she will need approximately 55 grams of protein daily (68 x 0.8 = 54.4 grams).

However, this is the minimum protein required to meet basic nutritional needs. Physically active women with certain health conditions or who are trying to lose weight may require more protein. Some experts recommend older adults may benefit from higher protein intake to help support muscle mass and function.

Make protein the star of your meals.

When it comes to nutrition, my best advice is JUST EAT REAL FOOD (JERF).

Avoid anything with an advert, anything containing over five ingredients, and anything with an element you can't pronounce. **If you're in a rush in the supermarket, stick to the outer aisles; that's where all the proper food hangs out.**

Great Protein-Rich Recipes

Grilled chicken with roasted vegetables: This dish is a classic protein-packed meal. Season chicken breasts with salt, pepper, and herbs, then grill until cooked. Serve alongside roasted vegetables like broccoli, carrots, and sweet potatoes.

Lentil soup: Lentils are an excellent source of plant-based protein. Make a hearty lentil soup by simmering lentils with vegetables like carrots, celery, and onions. Add some spices like cumin and turmeric for flavour and serve with a slice of crusty bread.

Tuna salad: Tuna is an excellent protein and omega-3 fatty acid source. Mix canned tuna with Greek yoghurt, celery, onion, and lemon juice for a healthy and flavourful tuna salad. Serve over a bed of greens or in a sandwich.

Quinoa bowl: Quinoa is a high-protein grain that makes an excellent base for a nutritious bowl. Top cooked quinoa with grilled chicken, roasted vegetables, avocado, and a drizzle of vinaigrette.

Greek yoghurt parfait: Greek yoghurt is a great source of protein and calcium. Layer Greek yoghurt with fresh fruit, granola, and a drizzle of honey for a healthy and satisfying breakfast or snack.

There are many more options, so don't be afraid to get creative in the kitchen! Also at the back of this book you'll find some great ideas for protein shakes: see Appendix 4 on page 133.

Fat

I want to clarify something about fat. Despite what we've been taught, fat is not bad for you. It's an essential nutrient for your body, providing "essential fatty acids." Your body needs fat to make hormones, repair tissue, and ensure your brain functions properly. Low-fat products often contain chemicals, so it's better to opt for the high-fat option. This way, you can also reduce your chemical intake.

Apple Cider Vinegar

I have been a loyal apple cider vinegar (ACV) fan for 25 years. I consume it every morning and even take it with me on holiday. First thing every morning, I drink a half-pint of water with ACV. When I first drank it I had to mix it with honey to balance the strong vinegar smell, but now I just drink it with water.

ACV is believed to help gut health because of its acetic acid, which stimulates the production of digestive enzymes and assists in breaking down food. Diluted ACV before meals may help ease symptoms like bloating or indigestion. Some people even find it helpful for acid reflux.

Research has shown that consuming ACV can help manage blood sugar levels, making it potentially useful for individuals with insulin resistance or type 2 diabetes. Some people find that taking ACV in warm water before bedtime helps prevent night-time trips to the bathroom, which may not always be because of bladder issues, but a drop in blood sugar levels. This method may be worth trying, as it can help stabilise blood sugar levels while you sleep.

There's also some research showing that ACV may aid in weight management by making you feel full and reducing your appetite. ACV may also promote a modest effect on metabolic rate and fat burning.

Am I convincing you to give it a go?

How Do Your Bowels Know You're On Holiday?

Have you ever noticed your bowels are affected when you're in an unfamiliar place, using a public loo, or just off your routine? Most women I know experience this. Women's bowels seem to be very sensitive to location. Men don't seem to have this issue; or at least, not the ones I've met.

Observation has shown that patients suffering from sciatica experience more pain when they need medication to help them go to the toilet. Hippocrates, the father of modern medicine, made this observation in ancient times. Recent research shows constipation is a significant cause of back pain, especially in women. Discomfort in the gut can lead to referred pain in the lower back because of the viscerosomatic convergence. This means your body hijacks the nerves in your lower back to signal that something is wrong. It's a similar mechanism to how a heart attack can cause pain in the left arm, because there are no nerves in the heart.

Experiencing pain in one part of your body can increase your sensitivity to pain in other areas.

Taking care of your gut health is crucial to ease back pain (see page 23).

Another thing to consider is that straining during bowel movements can put a lot of pressure on the lower spine muscles. This can significantly impact your spine health if it becomes a daily habit. A full colon can also affect the nerves in the lower back. Straining to pass a stool and holding it in can cause pressure on these nerves and lead to issues with your lower spine.

Taking care of bowel health is essential as it can significantly impact our overall health, especially for women with more sensitive bowels. Using the loo daily can even help ease back pain.

You may not have thought your back pain could be related to your bowel health, but it is worth considering. The frequency of healthy bowel movements can differ from person to person, and there's no one set standard for what's considered "healthy." Bowel movements between three times a week and three times a day are considered normal.

As women reach their 50s, it's common for their bowel movements to become less frequent than when they were younger. Diet, physical activity, overall health, and individual differences can influence this change. Unless you're experiencing discomfort, pain, or significant changes in bowel habits like sudden constipation or diarrhoea, there's usually no cause for concern. However, if you have specific concerns about your bowel movements or digestive health, it's always a good idea to consult with your GP.

My top tips for improving bowel health

1. Eat fermented foods such as kefir, kombucha, and sauerkraut—start including a few of these in your diet.
2. Eat a rainbow colour of foods.
3. Make sure you're getting plenty of fibre in your diet.
4. Aim for 30 different plants per week.
5. Drink plenty of water—2 litres per day.
6. Coffee first thing in the morning is excellent for starting the system.
7. Try to stick to a rhythm—bowels love the rhythm.
8. Massage your stomach (see Appendix 6 on page 139).
9. Drink some fruit juice (just a small glass if you're having problems).
10. Do some exercise; walking is a great way to get your bowels moving.
11. Add a daily dose of ACV.

Chapter 6

Why Your Bladder Health is Important for Back Pain

Did you know bladder health can be connected to back or pelvic pain?

The nerves shared by the bladder and lower back can become inflamed and irritated when the bladder is not working correctly. If the bladder is full or unable to empty, it can put pressure on the nerves in the lower back, leading to pain and discomfort. Bladder conditions, such as urinary tract infections or interstitial cystitis, can cause chronic pain in the lower back. These conditions can lead to inflammation in the bladder and surrounding tissues.

To prevent bladder infections, stay hydrated by drinking plenty of water and avoid irritants like caffeine and alcohol.

It's also important to maintain good hygiene practices.

Consider keeping a diary to track times you experience back pain and any potential connections to bladder, bowel, or pelvic pain. Note your bladder function during these times as well.

By doing pelvic floor exercises, you can strengthen the muscles that support your bladder and reduce the risk of urinary incontinence. The pelvic floor exercises demonstrated in the video[1] will aid in improving your bladder health.

The "Just In Case" Wee

We all know the drill—when heading out on a trip, or whenever we're out and about and spot a loo, we tend to use it even if we don't need to. However, doing so repeatedly can lead to bladder problems. Emptying your bladder before it's full can cause it to become less efficient at holding and releasing urine. This can cause frequent urination, sudden urges to pee, and even urinary leaks.

Frequent trips to the bathroom as a precautionary measure can cause us to hold urine for shorter durations, leading to bladder complications. This habit is called "key in the door syndrome," where the urge to urinate arises as soon as you put your key in the door when you arrive home. This is a product of associative and bladder/brain conditioning, like Pavlov's dogs. The sight of a toilet triggers the need to urinate (or the action of putting your key in the door).

Doing a "just in case" wee once or twice now and then won't harm you, but doing it frequently can create more problems for you in the long run. It is essential to listen to your body and only go to the toilet when necessary. This can help train your bladder to hold urine for extended periods and become more efficient at emptying.

Bladder/Brain Training

To start your bladder/brain training, pay attention to your body's signals. When you need to use the loo, hold it for a minute (or a time that feels comfortable). Take your time to go to the bathroom. Don't dash at the first signal. Instead, gradually increase the holding duration (equally, don't wait too long, as that can cause problems too). Make sure you're at home when trying this. It's important not to hold your urine mid-flow, as this can increase your risk of infection too.

Top Tips for Improving Bladder Health

- Drink plenty of water throughout the day to keep your urine diluted. This helps flush out bacteria and reduces the risk of urinary tract infections.
- Proper hygiene is crucial for preventing urinary tract infections. Always wipe from front to back after using the toilet to avoid transferring bacteria from the anal area to the urethra.
- Certain foods and beverages can irritate the bladder, leading to increased urination frequency or urgency. Limit or avoid caffeinated drinks, alcohol, spicy foods, and artificial sweeteners, as they can worsen bladder symptoms.
- Excess weight can put pressure on the bladder and pelvic muscles, leading to bladder control problems. Engage in regular physical activity and maintain a healthy weight to reduce the risk of urinary incontinence.
- Strengthening the pelvic floor muscles can help improve bladder control (see video).
- Smoking can irritate the bladder and increase the risk of bladder cancer. Quitting smoking

- not only benefits your overall health, but also promotes bladder health.
- If you have chronic conditions like diabetes or constipation, manage them effectively. These conditions can affect bladder health and increase the risk of urinary tract infections.
- Opt for cotton underwear and avoid tight-fitting clothing. Breathable fabrics allow air circulation and prevent moisture build-up, reducing the risk of bacterial growth and infections.
- Urinating before and after sexual activity helps flush out bacteria that may have entered the urethra during intercourse, reducing the risk of urinary tract infections.

You may not have considered that bladder health could be linked to your back pain. Keep your journal up to date on any issues with your bladder, what's irritated it, and what's triggered it—and it might give you some answers about your pain.

Again, if in any doubt, always consult your GP.

---

1. Don't forget to scan the QR code (on page 145) to get access to the free video series!

Chapter 7

The Pelvic Floor: What Is It, Where Is It, and Why Do We Need It?

We rarely talk about the importance of our pelvic floor (PF) muscles unless it is after giving birth. However, not all women learn how to do pelvic floor exercises after childbirth. My pelvic floor was severely damaged after my first delivery, to the point where walking was painful, and I had that awful bearing down feeling, like everything would fall out if I stood up or walked for too long.

I was told I need to do PF exercises, but I wasn't told how, and I wasn't even sure I knew where the PF was. That's when I started my own research. I studied, and I went on courses, and I learnt and practiced as much as I could. Three years later, when I had my second son, I was expecting the same problems, but when I was told I had to push, he was born super-quick. The midwife even commented that my PF was one of the strongest she'd seen, and she'd never delivered so fast. Right after birth, I was up on my feet and had none of the previous problems. That's how I knew my techniques had worked.

It's essential to keep in mind that your pelvic floor is a

collection of muscles that requires both strength and the ability to relax. Let's explore this further.

What the heck, and where the heck, is your pelvic floor?

(And why is it important when we're looking at how to reduce your back pain?)

In the "Anatomy of the Spine" section, we discussed the coccyx—a bone located at the base of the spine that can move slightly. The pelvic floor muscles attach to this bone, as well as to your sit bones and pubic bone. Imagine your sit bones on either side and your coccyx in the middle to visualise this. When you sit down, these three bones act like a tripod, helping you maintain proper posture and avoid slouching. Give it a try!

The PF muscles make a bowl shape in your pelvis and are the last line of defence from all your organs dropping out when you stand up. (Pelvic organ prolapse is a thing, which is a failure of the PF muscles.) Your PF muscles are unique as they need to be both strong to hold everything and must relax to let things out (your digestive system also requires your PF muscles).

To clarify, having equally strong and relaxed PF muscles is essential. When we say "relax," it doesn't mean the muscle is getting weaker, but that they are functioning correctly. We've learned to focus on contracting the muscles during pelvic floor exercises, but learning how to relax is equally important. That's where deep breathing and embodiment exercises come in.

We need to have a functioning PF—this means it needs to work and relax when needed. Why do I keep emphasising this point? You're about to find out, and it's super exciting and could hold the key to your back pain.

Intra-Abdominal Pressure

Managing the "pressures" within your body is essential to alleviating your back pain. Specifically, controlling your Intra-Abdominal Pressure (IAP) can be beneficial in addressing your back pain issues.

IAP is the "pressure in the abdominal cavity." This pressure is significant in creating stiffness and stabilising the lumbar spine.

Let's reconsider all that we know thus far:

1. Your PF muscles attach to your coccyx, your sit bones, and your pubic bone.
2. Your PF muscles must fully function to switch on (tone) and relax.

Researchers have found you can get a good idea of how healthy your pelvic floor muscles are by palpating your coccyx to see if it moves when you contract the pelvic floor.

And, yes, this does look like you're sticking your finger up your bum, but if you follow your spine down to the bottom, you can feel your coccyx. You're best to bend over whilst doing it, which will put your spine in a better place to feel it. Put your finger on your coccyx and try to pull up your PF—you'll feel it move slightly. Try to cough or laugh: if you can feel a slight movement there, then great; if not, it may mean you're holding onto the PF too much.

Also, remember in Chapter 3 on stress, I told you the PF muscles are one of the first to react to stress response? So, if you're in a stressed state, it means that your PF is activated, which as we now know, can lead to back and pelvic pain. Everything is connected. Reducing your stress levels means your PF can relax, and relaxing your PF shows your body that you feel safe, and switches on the PNS response.

Start by relaxing those muscles. Focus on the deep connection and relaxation—this is where breathing matters! We'll talk about this further in the next chapter.

Other Reasons for Pelvic Pain

Women have periods. Many women experience pelvic pain and cramping during menstruation, known as dysmenorrhea. The contractions of the uterus cause this pain as the uterus sheds its lining. If you're still having periods, it's a good idea to keep a diary or record of your pain symptoms tracked against your menstrual cycle. You may find some gold there as to when and where you may experience pain amplification.

Some other reasons you may experience pelvic pain:

Pelvic Inflammatory Disease (PID) is an infection of the female reproductive organs, often caused by sexually transmitted infections (STIs). It can lead to pelvic pain and other symptoms like abnormal vaginal discharge, fever, and pain during intercourse. Always get checked by a GP if you're in any doubt or experience new symptoms of this type.

Endometriosis is where the tissue lining the uterus (endometrium) grows outside the uterus. This can cause pelvic pain, especially during menstrual periods. It can also cause heavy periods, pain during intercourse, and infertility. Work with your GP for treatment plans, but I also know that combining good lifestyle factors will help you.

Ovarian cysts can develop on the ovaries and occasionally cause pelvic pain. Most cysts are benign and resolve independently, but larger cysts or those that rupture can cause significant pain.

Uterine fibroids are noncancerous growths that develop in the uterus. Depending on their size and location, they can cause pelvic pain, heavy menstrual bleeding, and pressure on nearby organs.

Pelvic organ prolapse occurs when the pelvic organs (such as the uterus, bladder, or rectum) descend or protrude into the vagina, causing pelvic pressure or pain.

Urinary tract infections (UTIs) are infections of the urinary tract, including the bladder and urethra. They can cause pelvic pain, along with symptoms such as frequent urination, burning sensation during urination, and cloudy urine.

Irritable bowel syndrome (IBS). It's not exclusive to women, but IBS is a digestive disorder that can cause abdominal pain, bloating, and changes in bowel habits, which may contribute to pelvic discomfort.

These are just a few potential causes, and pelvic pain can have various origins. Seek medical evaluation and advice to determine the specific cause of pelvic pain and develop an appropriate treatment plan.

It's no wonder we women suffer more from pelvic pain than men! Getting to the root of your pain will help to reduce the pain volume in your back and pelvis. If you are in any doubt, seek specialist guidance.

Castor Oil Packs

I love a natural remedy. Why waste all those years of ancient wisdom? We have used castor oil packs for centuries as a natural remedy to promote healing and relieve various types of pain, including pelvic pain. Castor oil contains ricinoleic acid, which has anti-inflammatory properties. Applying a castor oil pack to the pelvic area can help reduce inflammation and to relieve pain associated with pelvic inflammatory disease, endometriosis, or interstitial cystitis.

The castor oil pack creates a localised heat effect, which can help increase blood circulation to the pelvic region. Improved blood flow can bring oxygen and nutrients to the area, aiding healing and reducing pain.

The warmth from the castor oil pack, combined with its lubricating properties, can help relax the muscles in the pelvic area. This relaxation can alleviate muscle tension, spasms, and cramping, common causes of pelvic pain.

Castor oil packs are believed to have detoxifying effects. When applied to the skin, castor oil can penetrate deeper tissues, potentially eliminating toxins and waste products. Detoxification may help ease pelvic pain caused by toxic build-up or congestion.

To use a castor oil pack for pelvic pain, follow these steps:

1. Get a high-quality, cold-pressed castor oil and a piece of flannel or cotton cloth large enough to cover the pelvic area.
2. Fold the cloth into multiple layers, ensuring it is large enough to cover the entire pelvic region.
3. Generously saturate the cloth with castor oil but avoid making it dripping wet.
4. Lie on a comfortable surface, such as a bed or couch, and place the castor oil-soaked cloth over the lower abdomen and pelvic area.
5. Cover the pack with plastic wrap or a large bag to prevent staining.

6. Apply a heating pad or a hot water bottle on top of the pack to create warmth. Leave it in place for 30 minutes to 2 hours. You can use this time to relax, meditate, or listen to soothing music.
7. Afterwards, remove the pack and gently cleanse the skin with mild soap and warm water.

It's important to note that if you're pregnant, have an active infection, or have a known allergy to castor oil, avoid using castor oil packs.

Energy Flow into The Pelvic Bowl

It may sound "hippy" but many women I work with, who suffer from chronic back pain, tend to feel nothing in their pelvic area. It's like the entire area is shut down: it doesn't move, they can't feel anything, it's like there's a big gap between the upper and lower body. This area holds significant tension for women which can be attributed to various reasons, such as sexual trauma, birth, or pregnancy trauma. The pelvic region is linked to sexual energy and flow, affecting life's creativity, pleasure, and passions.

Although this is a complex topic, let's focus on directing energy into your pelvis and detecting blockages. In the exercise segment, we'll begin with pelvic tilting. Many women suffer from a stagnant pelvis that does not move. While performing pelvic tilts, synchronise them with your breathing. This will start the flow of energy (chi, prana, life-force energy, circulation—whatever you prefer to call it) into the region and encourage circulation. It's important that you feel safety in this area; many women don't. So, make sure you're breathing deeply, moving gently, and keeping your hands in contact with your hip bones and the pelvic area. This will help tell your nervous system that you are safe.[1]

The pelvic area is associated with the Sacral Chakra in the Chakra system (see Chakra Section). This chakra is linked to flow, the moon (like tides), and self-care. Consider how you bring pleasure and joy into your life. What are your passions? Are you living a life in alignment with your desires? I'll detail the Chakra system more later in the book.

Journaling these questions will help you come up with some answers. See the back of the book for all the journal prompts.

---

1. Watch the Week 1 video for more info on this.

Chapter 8

Why Breathing Matters to Your Back or Pelvis Pain, And Your Life

"Breath is the interconnecting link between your mind, spine and well-being."—Jill

Breath is your rhythm of your life. It's the first thing you do and the last. It's also one of the most important of the bodily functions, something your body is geared towards. I'm a Breathwork Teacher and Pilates Instructor, and this is where my two worlds collide into a beautiful, synergistic ball of energy.

The average person breathes 25,000 times per day. You can survive without food for roughly seven weeks and without water for around seven days. But the average person can only last for about seven minutes without oxygen. Oxygen is our primary fuel source, and our bodies cannot function correctly without it. It's a shame when I hear people say they've been breathing okay thus far in their lives, as there is always room for improvement in everything we do, including breathing. Unfortunately, we tend not to think about it for most of our lives, or ever!

As your breath is connected to various systems in your

body, including your stress response, digestive system, circulatory system, endocrine system, and more, it makes sense that managing your breath can positively impact these systems and your overall health.

Proper breathing techniques are essential for managing back pain and pelvic pain, both functionally and spiritually.

Breathing correctly is the most effective way for our bodies to release and manage pain naturally. It's why pregnant women are taught breathing techniques before giving birth. I always find it strange that people suffering from chronic pain are not also taught how to breathe correctly. It seems one area of the medical system recognises the power of breath for pain relief, yet they don't teach breathing techniques to everyone in pain.

Deep breathing stimulates the release of endorphins, our natural pain-relieving and mood enhancing hormones. Endorphins can help alleviate pain and induce feelings of well-being and relaxation. When you practice deep breathing, it helps to relax your muscles and removes tension from your body, and can also help to reduce anxiety and stress levels by calming the mind.

Breathing helps support the spinal column and drives intra-abdominal pressure (see last chapter) via your diaphragm—the breathing muscle at the bottom of your ribcage. The diaphragm has attachments right down into the lumbar spine, so breathing correctly can have effects right down your spine.

We know the stress response has two branches—the para-sympathetic response (PNS or rest and digest) and the sympathetic (SNS or fight or flight) response.

And here's the magic:

1. You can control those two responses via your breath.
2. You can only be in one state at a time.

Just ponder that for a moment.

When you intentionally slow down your breathing, this signals to your brain that you feel safe. It slows down your heart rate and blood pressure. This helps your body to remove stress hormones. You cannot simultaneously be in a fight-or-flight mode and a rest-and-digest mode. In Chapter 3, we learned stress and pain are inter-connected and can drive each other. Using your breath, you can help stop the upward spiral of pain and stress, calming your system, slowing your heart, and bringing yourself back into the PNS.

We also learned that your breath and pelvic floor are on the same neural loop, so correcting your breathing can help your pelvic floor function optimally. Everything is connected. If you close your eyes, sit up straight and tune into your pelvic floor, can you feel it activate slightly when you exhale, or maybe you can feel it on the inhale? Either way, every time you breathe, your pelvic floor activates too.

Breathing has a direct impact on your digestive system (the rest and digest response). Digestion is your body's second biggest energy user, after your immune system—both systems switch off when you're in a stressed state. That's why you get colds and low-level viruses when you're more stressed (ever notice this?) Consciously slowing down your breathing will help your body switch those two systems back on.

For now, I have a free ebook you can download from my website: www.organicpilates.co.uk.

When you begin a breathing practice, make sure you switch on your full body listening. This means you notice any tightness, restrictions, and pain in your body. Don't just focus on the pain; focus on where feels good, where feels safe, and the parts of your body you like.

Box Breathing is my favourite simple exercise to get you into a rest and digest mode quickly:

- Sit or lie down.
- Bring awareness to your bones, the ones touching the floor.
- Focus on your breath. As you exhale, make your bones feel heavy, almost melting into the floor.
- Relax your jaw.
- Bring more focus to the breath: allow your belly to expand and contract as you inhale and exhale.
- Feel your spine move naturally as you do this.
- Bring your attention to the breath—we're going to breathe in for a count of 4, hold for a count of 4, exhale for a count of 4, and hold for a count of 4. Imagine drawing a square in your mind as you do this.
- Start with a 5-minute practice and then build up.

You can also use this technique throughout the day to calm your stress and pain response should you feel triggered.

You will receive a video and I'll talk you through the process once you sign up via the QR code (on page 145).

Meditation or Breathwork?

Meditation has always been a challenge for me. When instructed to clear my mind, the opposite happens, and my thoughts run wild. However, practicing Breathwork helps me stay focused, as it gives my mind something to do, which switches it off.

The simplicity and transformative power of Breathwork amazes me.

If you're considering meditation or Breathwork practice, you don't need 30 minutes daily to sit still with candles and incense burning. I incorporate Breathwork into my daily activities, such as walking the dogs or driving. Simply becoming aware of your breathing, whether you are chest or belly breathing, and how it feels, can help you become more connected with your body and breath.

Use your breath as a guide. Trust your body, drop into yourself, and see how you feel. That will be enough.

Chapter 9

Why Sleep Is Your Biggest Pain Killer

"A well-spent day brings happy sleep." — Leonardo da Vinci

Sleep is one of my favourite subjects. It's so important to train yourself to sleep. As women age, we tend to suffer more sleep problems, especially with hormonal changes and bladder issues.

Two-thirds of adults throughout all developed nations fail to get the recommended 7-8 hours of sleep. Inadequate sleep affects your immune system, doubles your risk of cancer, increases your chances of getting Alzheimer's, and increases the likelihood of cardiovascular disease and many other health issues.

Getting to sleep and staying asleep is a superpower. In a recent survey, the two most reported sleep disturbances are too much caffeine during the day, or pets on the bed at night. If you're in either of those categories, then it doesn't take a rocket scientist to find the answers.

Sleep is when your brain recalibrates, and your whole body does a system reset. It's like your brain is going through a car wash (or a brainwash).

Pain and stress can directly impact the quality of your sleep. On the other hand, the amount of sleep you get can affect the pain and stress levels you experience. This can create a vicious cycle where pain keeps you awake, increasing pain and stress, and making sleeping even harder. It's easy to see how this cycle can be challenging to break.

So, how do you improve your sleep to improve your pain?

The relationship between breathing and sleep is closely intertwined. Proper breathing can aid with pain and stress management, and it can also promote better sleep. The quality of your sleep is influenced by the quality of your day, and ensuring good breathing habits throughout the day can also improve sleep quality.

Let's start with the basic things you can do throughout the day to help you get to sleep. Then we'll go into more specific breathing exercises to help, and I'll talk about mouth taping to help with sleep.

Circadian Rhythms

Humans are naturally inclined towards routine and are deeply connected to our environment. However, despite our 50,000 years of evolution, we have struggled to adapt to the rapid pace of industrialisation and digitalisation in the past century. While we are in sync with the natural rhythms of the sun, moon, and planet, our increasing reliance on digital technology has led to a disconnection from our innate nature. Unfortunately, this disconnection has resulted in various issues.

Our body functions best when our hormonal system and organs have a rhythm and flow. Therefore, aligning with these natural patterns is beneficial for our sleep and overall health.

There are two significant factors in getting to sleep at night—light and temperature.

But the quality of your sleep that night starts first thing in the morning.

Morning Routine

Start your day with some Yang (fire) energy by taking a cold shower, drinking caffeine, and soaking up the sun. This will help stimulate your natural hormonal wave and get your body firing on all cylinders. It's all about timing and finding the right systems to activate for a productive day ahead.

1. Get outside and look at the morning sun for 10 minutes to start your day. If it's cloudy, aim for 15 minutes instead. Being outside without sunglasses (regular glasses or contacts are okay) is essential to get the full benefits of the early morning light. This will jumpstart your hormonal system and give your body the light to start the day. It also helps to regulate your body clock.
2. Try taking a cold shower to wake up and energise your body. While it may seem counterintuitive, cold water raises your internal body temperature, providing a burst of energy to kick-start your day.
3. If you enjoy drinking coffee, it's best to have it in the morning to boost your energy for the day. However, if you want to get a good night's sleep, avoid consuming caffeine after noon.

4. Throughout the day, take time out to drop into your breath, just for a few minutes. How are you breathing? Can you slow your breath down? Breath awareness will help you become more embodied; your breath will tell you when you're stressed or calm.
5. Get outside during the day, especially if you work in an artificially lighted environment. Take a 15-20 min walk.
6. If you're a daytime napper (I know I am!), take at most 30 mins. Make sure it's early in the afternoon, so it's not disrupting your evening routine.
7. Hydrate—get enough water throughout the day; if I don't, it affects my sleep.
8. Get your pets out of your bed! I've got two big Labradors; no way would I be letting them sleep in my bed.

Evening Routine

1. Get outside in twilight—this does the reverse of the morning light.
2. Switch off devices at least 1 hour before you go to sleep.
3. Take a hot bath—this does the reverse of the cold shower and cools your core temperature.
4. Low-level lighting—avoid bright lights, especially fluorescent ones.
5. Avoid alcohol—although it will probably get you to sleep, it will cause you to wake up after a few hours. Plus, alcohol significantly reduces sleep quality.

6. Eat protein.

Supplements to help sleep:

- Avoid taking **melatonin** unless a doctor prescribes it. Melatonin plays multiple roles in the body; if you start taking it, your body may stop producing it naturally. Moreover, we don't fully understand how many different systems melatonin affects. Therefore, it is advisable not to interfere with it.
- **Cold, tart cherry juice** is the highest naturally produced melatonin you can get; it must be "tart" cherry juice, not the regular. Put it in your fridge and have a small glass just before you go to bed.
- **Magnesium threonine** is thought to be helpful; it's worth giving it a go. It also helps with aching joints. Make sure you take the correct dosage.

Breathing and Sleep

Breathing and sleep are closely related. Snoring and sleep apnoea are issues that affect breathing and can cause sleep problems. How you breathe while sleeping affects the quality of your sleep, just as how you breathe during the day activates specific functions in your body.

Difficulty falling asleep or staying asleep is insomnia, a prevalent sleep disorder affecting 25-30% of the general population.

Did you know that practising breathing techniques can improve insomnia? Researchers have discovered that incorporating breathing exercises into your daily routine and before bedtime can stimulate the body to produce more melatonin naturally. It can also activate the rest and digest section of the nervous system (PNS), and promote a calmer state. Studies have shown that breathing is more effective than traditional medication for insomnia.

There is a strong connection between breathing difficulties and stress and anxiety. This can lead to sleep disorders, and the reverse is also true.

When you breathe rapidly during the day, your sympathetic nervous system (SNS) becomes activated and remains hyper-aroused throughout the night. This can lead to increased alertness, panic attacks, and anxiety, which often result in amplified worries and stress at night. A hyperactive SNS during the day can also carry over into the night-time.

How to sleep better through better breathing:

1. Place one hand on your belly and one hand on your chest. Slow your breathing, expand into your stomach on the inhale, and contract on the exhale. Do this for 15 mins.
2. Breath holds: I like this gentle breath-holding technique to help with sleep. Begin by slowing your breath and taking it deep into your belly. Try to make your breath so light that you can't feel it entering your nose; if you were to put a feather in front of your nose, you wouldn't move it. This is called LSD Breath (Light, Slow, Deep). Then, on an exhale, suspend your breath for a count of 6 (or whatever number feels good for you), then do two LSD breaths and continue with the suspension.

Mouth Taping

When you wake up with a dry mouth, it could be a sign that you breathe through your mouth while sleeping. This habit can increase the risk of gum disease, bad breath, and tooth decay, compared to breathing through your nose. Mouth breathers may also experience stress more frequently, and their stress response can activate faster. Training yourself to breathe through your nose is crucial, as it is the correct way to breathe, as nature intended. It has various health benefits, including improving sleep quality. In James Nestor's book, he explains that sleep issues can be related to breathing problems.

Did you know you can train your body to breathe through your nose at night using a special tape called MyoTape? Tape your mouth shut before bed, and your body will naturally adjust to nasal breathing. If you do this consistently for one week, your body will become accustomed to it. To maintain this healthy habit, repeat the process for a week every few months if you slip back into bad breathing habits. And, yes, it may also help with snoring husbands!

Even though it may seem strange, taping your mouth shut at night can have several benefits. Breathing through your nose during sleep helps filter, warm, and humidify the air, reducing dryness or irritation in your airways. Nasal breathing also promotes the production of nitric oxide, a gas with various physiological functions, including dilating blood vessels and enhancing oxygen use. Mouth taping keeps your mouth closed while you sleep, encouraging nasal breathing, which is believed to be the best way to improve sleep quality and respiratory health overall.

Mouth breathing at night can cause the tongue to rest at the bottom of the mouth, adversely affecting oral and dental health due to improper tongue posture. Mouth taping can help by encouraging the tongue to rest against the roof of the mouth, which supports proper tongue posture and potential benefits for oral health.

If you have chronic nasal congestion, sleep apnoea, or respiratory disorders, consult a healthcare professional before attempting mouth taping.

Nitric Oxide (NO)

(Not to be confused with Nitrous Oxide (N2O)—laughing gas.)

Nasal breathing has the significant advantage of optimising nitric oxide production in your body. Nitric oxide is a natural molecule that acts as a vasodilator. It helps to relax the blood vessels, promote proper blood flow, and enhance overall health.

When researchers first discovered nitric oxide, they observed an interesting side effect which led to the creation of Viagra. Nitric oxide also has various other benefits, such as aiding muscle soreness, reducing blood pressure, improving exercise performance, and potentially assisting in treating type 2 diabetes.

The largest production area of nitric oxide is behind the nasal cavity. Therefore, when you inhale through your nose, you directly breathe it into your lungs. If you slow down your breath, it accumulates in your nasal cavity, and you can breathe it in more effectively.

Here are another of my two favourite breathing techniques to bring about calm:

NSDR Protocol (Non-Sleep Deep Rest)

I first heard this on Andrew Huberman's podcast. This one is for if you can't get to sleep but want to feel deeply rested.

1. Lying on your back, imagine you're standing on your feet with a torch in your hand.
2. You shine your beam onto your right foot.
3. Focus all your attention on that foot. Where is it holding onto tension? Anywhere feeling any pain? Can you relax more?
4. Then move to the other foot. Does it feel the same? What are the differences between your two feet?
5. Gradually move up legs, right then left.
6. Then shine the light over both of your legs; how do they feel together?
7. Move up the whole body.
8. When at the top of the head, shine a light on the entire body.
9. If required, move back down, starting at the head.

CCB through the nose (Conscious Connected Breathing)

CCB, or circular breath, is a breathing technique I teach in my Breathwork sessions to alter consciousness and go into a dreamlike state. I usually teach it through the mouth, which can be energising, but practising it through your nose becomes more soothing. Here's how to do it:

1. Lying down, pull air in through your nose, right down into your tummy.

2. Just let go on the exhale through your nose.
3. Remove any pauses.
4. Keep the pattern circular.

Do this for 5/10 minutes or until you fall asleep.

Practice these as well as Box Breathing and LSD breathing. You will also receive audio versions of these techniques when you sign up with the QR code (on page 145).

Chapter 10

Hello, Hormones!

In writing a book about women and back/pelvic pain, I would be remiss not to mention the significant role women's hormones can play. Hormonal changes during the menstrual cycle, pregnancy, and menopause can affect the musculoskeletal system and contribute to pain.

Some women experience lower back pain and pelvic discomfort during their menstrual cycle because of the relaxing effect of oestrogen and progesterone on the ligaments and muscles in the pelvic area. This can cause instability and strain on the lower back and through the pelvis.

Pregnancy results in significant hormonal changes to prepare for giving birth. One hormone, called relaxin, relaxes the ligaments and joints in the pelvis and lower back. Although this increases flexibility, it can also lead to instability and strain on the spine, causing discomfort and back pain.

As women go through menopause, their oestrogen levels decrease, which can cause osteoporosis. This condition weakens bones and puts individuals at a higher risk for fractures in the spine and other body parts. The ligaments and supporting structures in the body can weaken, leading to joint pain.

If you are in perimenopause, which can begin in your 40s, it is crucial to monitor your cycle. Pay attention to any patterns related to your back pain. Does it intensify during ovulation or your period? Do you experience more pain at certain times of the month? Note your sleep patterns during these times. Are you craving more sugar?

Understanding your body and menstrual cycle can provide valuable information to help you plan accordingly. If you know the days when you will experience more pain or less sleep, you can plan your work schedule around them.

Regular exercise can help balance hormones and strengthen the muscles in your spine. Research shows that any form of physical activity is effective, so find a practice that works for you and incorporate it into your routine. Walking, swimming, and Pilates are all great options to consider. The best exercise is the one you'll do!

Taking care of your stress levels is essential, as chronic stress can disrupt hormone balance and lead to pain. Various practices, such as meditation, deep breathing, and progressive muscle relaxation, can help reduce stress and induce relaxation.

A healthcare professional may suggest hormone replacement therapy to balance hormones and ease back pain. However, seek their guidance as HRT can have potential risks and side effects.

A Note on Your Adrenal Glands

Knowing about the adrenal glands is essential, especially as we age. When women go through menopause, which usually happens between ages 45 and 55, the ovaries produce fewer hormones like oestrogen and progesterone. But other glands, such as the adrenal glands, play a more significant role.

The adrenal glands are small triangular-shaped glands on top of each kidney. Their primary function is to produce different hormones, such as cortisol, aldosterone, and dehydroepiandrosterone (DHEA). Particularly during menopause, the adrenal glands play a crucial role in hormone production and balance.

Notice cortisol in that list? When you reach menopause, and your ovaries stop producing sex hormones, your adrenals take over some of the production. However, if you're stressed and not managing the stress well, your adrenals will favour cortisol over sex hormones. Your body prioritises stress hormones over sex hormones for survival.

Many women face challenges during menopause, which I believe can be attributed to the body's complex and finely balanced systems. Menopausal symptoms are common, but they're not normal. Although the body has natural mechanisms to aid us, these systems malfunction when we subject ourselves to continuous stress.

Why you need to show your adrenals some love:

- Once menopause occurs, and the ovaries cease producing oestrogen, the adrenal glands still produce small levels of androgens, including DHEA. These androgens can be transformed into oestrogen in peripheral tissues like fat cells. This conversion in peripheral tissues is vital in sustaining an appropriate level of oestrogen in the body, which is necessary for multiple physiological processes.

- The adrenal glands work closely with the ovaries and other endocrine glands to ensure a balanced hormonal system. When the ovaries reduce their hormone production, the adrenal glands take over to maintain the proper balance of hormones in the body, including oestrogen, progesterone, and testosterone.
- The body's stress response is influenced by the adrenal glands, which produce cortisol when faced with stressors. In menopause, when women undergo hormonal changes and experience physical and emotional changes, the adrenal glands help regulate the stress response and mitigate its effects on the body.

During menopause, the adrenal glands assist in hormone production, but they cannot fully replace the hormones lost from the ovaries. Menopause causes complex hormonal changes and symptoms involving multiple body systems. However, allowing the adrenal glands to function properly can help ease many of these symptoms.

To look after your adrenals, reduce stress and eat a diet that includes fruits, vegetables, whole grains, and lean protein.

Proper sleep is crucial for hormone regulation and your adrenals.

Chapter 11

Alcohol—Where Angels Fear to Tread

At the time of writing, I've got a year and a half without alcohol, and it's been one of the best things I've done for my health. Until you stop drinking, you don't even notice how much of your life is governed by it. I know many won't want to hear this, and I would have included myself in this a couple of years ago.

Women and alcohol are so intertwined with each other that stepping out of that matrix can be tricky. You may think that glass of wine on a Friday night is well-deserved, and what harm can a couple of drinks on a Saturday afternoon do? How about that large glass of wine with your Sunday lunch? I know because that was me, too. I wasn't a big drinker, but I was a regular one.

When I stopped drinking alcohol, I noticed how ingrained it is in our society: everything revolves around drinking. On TV, in every drama show, the first thing professional women do on screen is reach for the wine bottle as soon as they get home. Watch out for it; you'll notice it now.

I will not tell you to quit drinking altogether like I did,

as it must be a personal choice. What I am going to say is you must make an informed decision if you continue to drink alcohol whilst trying to heal your pain. Alcohol is a poison to your body; there is no other word for it. Whilst you are trying to eat healthily and make positive lifestyle changes, reducing or quitting alcohol must be one of the best things that you can do for your body, and I speak from personal experience.

Here are some other reasons to quit the drink:

- As women age, our bodies become more vulnerable to certain health conditions. Excessive alcohol consumption can increase the risk of developing conditions such as liver disease, osteoporosis, heart disease, and certain types of cancer.
- Women over 50 are more likely to take multiple medications to manage various health conditions. Alcohol can interact negatively with certain medications, diminishing their effectiveness or causing harmful side effects.
- Menopause brings about hormonal changes in a woman's body. Alcohol can exacerbate menopausal symptoms such as hot flashes and mood swings, ruining sleep.
- As we age, our bodies metabolise alcohol more slowly. This means the effects of alcohol can be more pronounced and prolonged in older individuals, leading to increased impairment and potential health risks.
- Women have a lower tolerance for alcohol compared to men because of differences in body composition and enzyme production. This means even moderate amounts of alcohol can

have a more substantial impact on women over 50.

Plus, alcohol can directly interfere with some of the areas that we're trying to improve. These are things you may not have considered:

- Pain is your body's way of signalling that something is wrong. Alcohol can mask or temporarily numb pain, leading you to ignore or overlook potentially underlying severe issues. It's essential to address the root cause of the pain rather than relying on alcohol to alleviate symptoms.
- Alcohol can interfere with the body's natural healing processes. It can impair the immune system, delay tissue repair, and hinder the body's ability to recover from injuries or surgeries. Drinking alcohol while in pain may impede healing and prolong recovery.
- Pain itself can affect coordination and reaction times. Adding alcohol can further impair motor skills, judgment, and decision-making abilities. This increases the risk of accidents, falls, and injuries, particularly if you are already experiencing pain or taking pain medication.
- Alcohol is a depressant that can exacerbate sadness, anxiety, or depression. If you are already in pain, alcohol can negatively impact your emotional well-being, leading to increased emotional distress or difficulties coping with pain.

If you are serious about healing your pain and

improving your health, then you must discuss and consider your alcohol use.

I gave up drinking by starting with dry January. I managed a month and kept going—and never looked back. You may need extra support around this, depending on how much you drink. If you can do it alone, take it one day at a time. If you do need extra support, speak to a medical specialist.

Chapter 12

What Types of Exercise Should I Do?

When it comes to exercise, like nutrition, things can get overcomplicated. There's so much advertising and new exercise programs coming out that you get paralysis by analysis and end up doing nothing. Please keep it simple!

The best exercise for you is the one that you find enjoyable.

Based on my teaching experience, people are more likely to continue with things they find fun. You are less likely to stick with a particular exercise if you don't enjoy it. I don't like running or jogging; you will never find me doing it. However, I enjoy walking. Even though running is a great calorie burner, I won't do it. I love strength training; give me a kettlebell or a weight, and I'm all there. I love the feeling I get after a great session with the iron.

You must find out what works for you.

There are some fundamentals, though, especially for women. Firstly, keeping your joints healthy requires mobility training.

Why You Need Mobility Training

We spend a lot of time sitting or standing, being in the same posture. Your joints need to move through their full range to stay happy, mobile, and well oiled. Mobility training gives you flexibility, stability, and overall movement quality. During menopause, lots of women experience joint pain, which is down to not moving correctly and the muscles holding the joints becoming weak.

A tree that bends is less likely to break; the same is true of our joints. Being more mobile reduces your risk of injury should you slip or fall. You're also able to stay active, take part in sports or recreational activities, and age well.

Strength Training—Women Need Iron

Swinging a kettlebell is something I love to do. When we reach our 50s, we need strength training. In my book (which this is!) it's non-negotiable. As we age, we experience a natural loss of muscle mass known as sarcopenia. Strength training helps counteract this muscle loss by promoting muscle growth. It stimulates bone growth and increases bone mineral density, reducing the risk of osteoporosis and fractures.

If you want to lose some weight, the kettlebells are your friend. Strength training increases metabolic rate, so once you build muscle you can eat the same number of calories but burn more, as muscles require energy. Building lean muscle mass increases calorie expenditure, even at rest, thus counterbalancing the natural slow-down with age.

Research has proven that strength training positively affects hormonal balance and general health. It can aid in regulating hormones like oestrogen and insulin, enhance mood, alleviate stress, and boost energy levels. Weight training can reduce hot flushes by 50%.

If you're new to resistance training, make sure you do so with proper form and technique. It may be worth getting a few private lessons, and you must increase your weights and intensity gradually.

Why is Muscle the Longevity Organ?

Muscle is our real anti-ageing secret.

Muscle is a crucial factor in healthy ageing and in slowing down age-related decline. The health of muscles and bones is interlinked. As we get older, our metabolic rate slows down, causing a decrease in calorie expenditure. However, having more muscle mass can help maintain a healthy metabolic rate, which promotes better weight management and overall metabolic health.

Strong muscles help us maintain balance, stability, and mobility, which makes everyday activities like walking, climbing stairs, or carrying groceries much easier. It maintains our independence.

Our posture may decline as we get older. Building and preserving muscle will help to improve posture. This can lead to a more youthful and healthy appearance.

Chapter 13

The Plan of Action and Why You Need To Train

"Change is never painful. Only the resistance to change is painful."
Buddha

Dealing with back and pelvic pain requires a comprehensive approach. It's not a quick fix, but a journey requiring gradual changes and patience. Attempting too much too soon will only lead to failure.

I have recorded videos of all the exercises and some Breathwork exercises for you to follow. I recommend doing one week at a time, and I've included my suggested lifestyle habits for each week. It's crucial to determine what works best for you and discover your recipe for success, so please be patient and prepare for a lot of trial and error.

Every week, you will receive three exercises to concentrate on. It will only take five minutes to complete them every day. Watch the instructional videos to ensure you use the proper techniques and breathing for each exercise. Some exercises may be enjoyable and suit you, while others may be more challenging. Try all of them because the more challenging practices are often the ones you need the most.

Please note you must have your whole body listening switched on whenever you exercise. DO NOT FORCE your body to do anything; if it doesn't feel right for you, it probably isn't.

You need a clear area for exercising. Ensure all trip hazards, candles, cups, small children, dogs, and cats are out of the room. All exercises are done at your own risk, so please ensure you stay safe, and if in any doubt, consult your GP.

QR Code

When you sign up using the QR code below, I'll send you a weekly video with demonstrations of all the exercises.

Point your phone camera at the QR code and you'll be taken to the site, or alternatively sign up here:

https://organic-pilates-holistic-health.ck.page/93b5645e36

Week 1: Understanding Your Lumbar Spine and Pelvic Floor

"You are not who you are now. You are who you are who you are becoming."—Carl Jung

We are going to get you moving using very simple but effective movements.

Week 1 is all about finding your core and getting your lower back moving.

Please remember to have your full body listening switched on, and to check with your GP if you're in any doubt if you should be exercising. All exercises are done at your own risk.

Exercises

- **Pelvic Tilts**: lie on the floor with your knees bent and start to flatten your spine to the floor, then tilt it the other way. Start off gently, then gradually make your movements bigger.

- **Pelvic Floor Awareness**: bring your awareness to the base of your spine and your sphincter muscles, contract gently. Then bring awareness to your vaginal muscles, then contract those gently. Then your urethra muscles (where you wee from), and contract those gently. Those three areas hold the PF muscles—start to contract all three together like pulling three strings up to your bellybutton. Then relax them. Combine this with your breath. Inhale, exhale—contract your muscles. Inhale exhale—relax them.
- **Heel Slides**: tilt your pelvis again and find a position where your lumbar spine is lifted slightly from the floor. You should be able to post a letter under. Then on an exhale slowly slide your heel away from you. Keep the heel gently touching the floor. And slide it back in to swap sides. Exhale to slide away, inhale to slide back and swap.

Habits to Focus on This Week

This week we're easing ourselves into our new healthy lifestyle. This is what I want you to focus on:

1. Drink enough water, around 2L per day. Remember a healthy spine is a fully hydrated spine (if you don't drink enough water your body will take water from your inter-vertebral discs or the poo waiting in your colon. You don't want to be powered by poo water!)

2. Move everyday: do little and often. Just 5 mins a day of the exercises.
3. Walking is one of the best things to do for your spine, make sure you're getting outside for a brisk 20 min walk each day.

Week 2: Segmental Control of Your Spine

We are going to start moving into the different areas of your spine and get your spine moving a little bit more.

Week 2 is all about getting our WD40 out, and oiling some of those joints.

Please remember to have your full body listening switched on, and to check with your GP if you're in any doubt if you should be exercising. All the exercises are done at your own risk.

Exercises

- **Pelvic Tilts into a gentle bridge**: begin with your pelvic tilts like we did last week. Start to peel your spine off the floor, vertebrae by vertebrae. Go slowly and gently, do one vertebra then return, then next time do another one, keep going until you are in a bridge position.

- **Knee Pulls**: lie on your back, gently pull one knee into your chest, hold for 10 secs. Exhale and switch legs.
- **Tick Tock Knees**: lie on your back with your knees bent, gently sway your knees side to side, imagine a tick tock sound in your head.

Habits to Focus on This Week

This week we're building on last week's habits. Let's start to think about the food that we're putting into our bodies—are we fuelling for success?

Re-read Chapter 5 on nutrition and see if you can begin to make some good changes.

If you're stuck for recipes, go to my website www.organicpilates.co.uk/shop where you'll find a high-protein recipe pack to buy which will be great for accompanying your healthy spine.

Plus, at the back of this book I've included a 30 Plant Challenge: see if you can get as many different plants into your diet as possible over a week.

Week 3: Your Thoracic Spine and Shoulders

This week we're heading into another problem area for women: the upper back and shoulders. As we age and our hormones start to decrease, we lose strength and elasticity in our upper back and shoulders. Of course, we've had a lifetime of carrying our boobs around which in some cases can be very heavy! And wearing bras, too.

By the way—when was the last time you got fitted for a bra? It might be worth having a refit—you might be surprised at the difference it makes to your comfort levels.

Working on the upper back and shoulder muscles can help to decrease pain in this area, and also improve posture.

Exercises

- **Dart:** Lie on your front, face down, arms by your sides with your palms facing upward. Keeping your head in line with your spine, inhale and as you exhale gently raise your chest off the floor, whilst squeezing your shoulder blades together. Hold for a couple of seconds, and then return to the floor on an inhale. Repeat x 8.

- **Threadneedle:** Go onto all fours, turn your fingers to face each other. Push one arm through the other, taking your whole shoulder girdle with you until you're twisting through. Return and repeat on the other side.
- **Tabletop:** Start on all fours, exhale and reach out one arm and the opposite leg. Lift them in line with your spine and see if you can hold for a few seconds. Return to centre and repeat on other side.

Habits for this week

Re-read Chapter 9 on sleep—let's see if you can start getting 7-8 hours uninterrupted sleep every night.

Journal about how your spine and pelvis are feeling, and note your pain levels.

Week 4: All About Your Hips

Your hips don't lie, as Shakira once said! This week we're looking at hip mobility and how we can increase and improve our range. Lower back pain and hip mobility are closely connected.

Once we get your hips moving it will start to free up your lower back. You may also find that your knee and ankle health begin to improve as well. Your hips are the bridge between your upper and lower body, so they are key to getting your body moving and grooving again.

Exercises

- **Hip Circles:** Lie on your back, knees bent. Extend one leg straight upwards. Start circling the leg from the hip. Do small circles to start, then gradually make them bigger. Do around 8-10 repetitions, then change direction. Repeat on other leg.

- **Oyster:** Lie on your side with knees bent, feet in line with the hips. Make sure your hips are stacked. Slowly start to open the leg, making sure your hips don't rock backwards. Do 8-10 repetitions, then repeat on the other side.
- **Squats:** I LOVE squats. Don't worry, we'll start off small then work to your own level.

Habits for the week

Let's start introducing some breathing exercises into your life.

Re-read Chapters 3 and 8 about managing your stress and breathing.

Week 5: Strengthening the Lower Back

A lot of lower back pain is due to weakness, so this week we're looking at some lumbar spine strengthening exercises, plus introducing some "Primal Patterns". Primal Patterns are movements we should be able to do naturally as humans: they are squat, bend, lunge, twist, push, and pull.

Exercises

- **Dead bug:** Lie on your back with arms and legs in the air (knees at right angles). Extend one arm and the opposite leg out straight, then return. Modification: keep feet on the floor and extend heel away instead of lifting the leg. Do each side 8-10 times.
- **Supermans:** Lie on your front with arms extended (as if you were flying like Superman). Slowly exhale and raise your arms and legs off

the floor. Modification: just lift the arms, then replace, then lift the legs. Repeat 8-10 times.

- **Lunges:** Standing upright, take a big step forward, bend both your knees until the back one almost touches the floor. Return and repeat on the other leg. Do this 8-10 times for each leg. Modification: hold onto a chair or surface for stability.

Habits for the week

Let's make a start on improving your gut health—read Chapter 5 on nutrition and gut health. Start including some fermented foods into your diet.

Week 6: Putting It All Together

We've come a long, long way together. If you've been following along with the program, you should be feeling the benefits by now. This week is all about putting together a little routine or choosing a few exercises you can do a couple of times a week.

Here's a suggested routine for you (I'll do this in the video):

- Warm Up Exercises: standing upright in good posture, breathing exercises, standing on one leg, then the other.
- Squats or lunges (or both).
- Lying on back: pelvis tilts into shoulder bridges, heel slides, tick tock knees, hip circles, dead bug.
- Lying on side: Oyster.
- Four-Point Kneeling: Table top, Threadneedle.
- Lying on front: Dart and Superman.
- Finish with some deep breathing exercises.

You should now have embedded lots of the habits into your lifestyle, too.

How are you feeling?

Make sure you journal regularly and keep up with your practice.

Do let me know how you are getting on.

Chapter 14

Mindset and Energy

"Whether you think you can or you can't, you're correct."
—Henry Ford

Your mindset is your superpower. Are you ready to start working on yourself? If so, great! Working on yourself is a long-term commitment to personal growth and expansion.

If you still need more time to prepare, that's okay too. You must begin when you're ready and the time is right for you.

Research shows that negative emotions and stress can increase pain sensitivity and slow healing. On the other hand, a positive mindset can enhance pain tolerance and speed up recovery. By developing a positive attitude, we can harness the power of the mind-body connection and boost our body's natural healing abilities.

Recovering from back or pelvic pain can be a complex process that involves medical treatment, physical therapy, lifestyle changes, and self-care practices. Maintaining a positive outlook is essential to stay motivated and committed to the programme. This optimistic attitude can help build confidence in the possibility of recovery. It can encourage perseverance, even during slow progress or setbacks.

How to Build a Positive Mindset

There will be days when you feel like crap; that's life. Building a positive mindset means you'll understand that you'll have days like these. But you also know you'll have great days, knowing that things will improve. Watch your language on bad days; ensure you're not perpetuating the pain. Remember, every cell in your body listens to what you're saying.

Knowledge of your condition is crucial to alleviate any fear or uncertainty and make informed decisions regarding your health. Please don't blindly believe everything I say. Do your research.

Using visualisation techniques can be so helpful. Envision life without pain, picture your back healing and enjoying activities that make you happy. Allow yourself to be in the present moment without judgement, sit with your body, and ask what it needs. Emotions are Energy in Motion—so know that your emotions are just passing through you; they won't always be there; in fact, they've usually changed by the next day.

Following your doctor's orders is vital, but gentle exercises like walking or stretching can enhance blood flow, decrease rigidity, and stimulate endorphins, which are natural painkillers. Engaging in physical activity can also positively impact your mindset and overall health.

Remember, building a positive mindset takes time and consistent effort. It's essential to be patient and compassionate with yourself throughout the process.

Keeping track of your progress, emotions, and plans to stay on course in your journal will help keep you on track. Remember, some days will be fantastic, with glimpses of a life without pain, while others will have setbacks. The healing process is not a straight line, but your commitment and persistence will help you persevere.

Just KEEP GOING!

Attitude of Gratitude

It's hard to think about anything else when you're in pain. However, if you consciously practice gratitude, you can redirect your attention towards the positive aspects of your life. Doing so can help you achieve balance and perspective and shift your focus from the pain. Gratitude is also a high vibrational emotion.

Cultivating gratitude has been found to have many benefits, including increased positive emotions, improved overall well-being, and reduced stress levels. By consciously acknowledging and appreciating the positive aspects of your life, you can experience feelings of joy, contentment, and happiness. These emotions can help counteract the negative impact of pain and improve your overall mood and outlook.

Practising gratitude can help you be more mindful and accept the present moment. Recognising and being thankful for the good things in your life, you learn to take positive and negative experiences. This can help you develop resilience, better manage pain, and find purpose and worth in challenging situations.

Being grateful for those who support, care, and understand you can enhance your relationships and social connections. It creates a sense of connection and encourages a supportive network around you. A strong support system can offer emotional comfort, understanding, and distraction from pain.

Acknowledging the good things in your life can improve your outlook and lead to a more positive mindset. By focusing on the positives, you can develop hope and believe things will improve. This can help you become more resilient, motivate you to manage any pain you may experience, and boost your confidence in your ability to cope and find relief.

Your attitude of gratitude helps when you integrate it with all your other healthy lifestyle habits. Every day, think of three things you're grateful for as soon as you wake up and last thing at night.

Affirmations: What Are They and How Can They Help?

Affirmations can be a valuable tool: they can also aid in pain management by positively affecting your emotional state and overall well-being. Affirmations are straightforward, positive statements you can repeat to yourself regularly. Redirect your attention from negative thoughts to more positive and empowering ones by including affirmations in your daily routine.

By repeating affirmations that focus on relief, comfort, and healing, you can develop a more positive perception of your pain. This can help reduce the stress and anxiety associated with pain, enabling you to manage your symptoms better.

Living with chronic pain can affect your emotional health, leading to feelings of frustration, anger, or sadness. However, practising affirmations can help boost your emotional well-being by fostering positive emotions and self-compassion. Repeating affirmations that encourage self-love, acceptance, and resilience can help you achieve greater emotional balance and enhance your overall mood.

By acknowledging your strength, perseverance, and ability to manage pain, you can empower yourself to approach challenges proactively. These affirmations remind you of your inner resources and capacity to navigate pain, keeping you motivated and resilient.

Repeating affirmations that promote relaxation, comfort, and well-being can enhance the mind-body connection, which is crucial for managing pain. This positive influence on physiological responses can reduce muscle tension, stress, and other physical symptoms associated with pain.

How to Write an Affirmation

Keep them simple. If you want to reduce your pain, write something like:

"Today I am giving my body what it needs to heal."

Or: "I will hydrate my body," "I am feeling amazing today," "I am worthy of love," or "I love my body."

Don't put the word "pain" into your affirmation; just keep thinking, what do I want to amplify? If you use the word "pain" that's what will get amplified!

Repeat affirmations regularly, preferably multiple times daily, to reinforce positive beliefs and thoughts.

Visualise the affirmations and connect with the emotions they evoke to enhance their effectiveness.

Affirmations are another tool to add to your toolkit when you're ready. Please give them a go; they will not harm you.

Every Cell in Your Body is Listening—Your Biography Becomes Your Biology

Dr Bruce Lipton is a renowned cellular biologist and author known for his work in epigenetics. He proposes that our thoughts, beliefs, and perceptions can influence our biology and overall health by altering the expression of our genes. This concept challenges the conventional understanding that our genetic makeup solely determines our health outcomes.

His book, *The Biology of Belief*, explores the relationship between mind and body, highlighting the role of perception and consciousness in shaping our physical well-being. He suggests that our beliefs can act as an "epigenetic control" that can activate or deactivate specific genes, ultimately influencing our health and life experiences.

For me, his work emphasises that every cell in your body is listening, and by positively changing your mindset and how you talk to yourself, you will change your body at a cellular level. It's fascinating stuff. I recommend reading the book if you want to go deeper into it.

Energy: Building and Maintaining It

> *"Everything is energy, and that's all there is to it. Match the frequency of the reality you want, and you cannot help but get that reality. It can be no other way."*—Einstein

The Scientific Definition

Energy is the force that enables physical and mental activities in the human body and is vital for the proper functioning of our systems. In the scientific context, energy is a fundamental concept in physics, defined as "the ability to cause change or do work."

Energy exists in various forms and can be converted from one form to another. The common forms of energy include kinetic, potential, chemical, thermal, electrical, light, and sound energy.

Energy is necessary for all bodily processes, such as muscle contractions, nerve impulses, metabolism, and organ and system function. The body gains energy by consuming and breaking down food into molecules that create adenosine triphosphate (ATP), the primary currency for cell energy.

Why We Need Energy for Our Body to Function Correctly (The Science Version)

Managing pain effectively involves understanding energy's critical role. This is because both physiological and psychological factors impact pain perception and response, many of which are related to energy systems within your body.

Neurons communicate through electrical impulses that rely on energy-generating processes. Sufficient energy availability is crucial for the nervous system to function correctly and transmit pain signals. A proper energy supply supports the healing of injured tissues and can help alleviate pain associated with tissue damage or inflammation.

You cannot relax without energy. Think about that one!

Life Force Energy (The Juicy Bit)

The concept of life force energy, which goes by different names such as chi, prana, or vital energy, is present in various ancient healing systems and spiritual traditions. It is described as a subtle energy or vital force that gives life and sustains it. We don't have a word in English that directly describes it. It's ethereal, but it's there. Although it is not widely recognised or studied by the scientific community, it remains significant in cultural, spiritual, and alternative healing practices.

Various traditions have different interpretations of life force energy. Still, they all agree it's a subtle, non-physical force that runs through living beings and affects physical, emotional, and spiritual well-being. It's often described as a pervasive energy encompassing the entire body or the environment.

In traditional Chinese medicine, the life force energy is "chi" and is believed to flow through meridians or energy pathways in the body. When the flow of chi is disrupted or imbalanced, it's thought to cause physical or emotional disturbances. Practices such as acupuncture, qigong, or tai chi aim to restore the balanced flow of chi.

In Indian ayurvedic medicine and yoga, life force energy is called "prana." It's believed to be the energy that sustains all life processes and practices such as pranayama (breathing exercises) and specific yoga postures aim to balance and enhance the flow of prana.

How to Build Your Energy

"You are not your age, you are your energy."

Maintaining high levels of energy is a full-time task. People often ask me how I have so much energy. The secret is that I'm excellent at resting. It's all about Yin and Yang. My job requires a lot of energy, as I teach daily Pilates classes and clients, manage a business, and have teenagers and Labradors.

All require energy!

Not only do I need it in abundance, but I'm also cautious about protecting my energy.

To have high energy levels, it's essential to establish healthy lifestyle habits that cater to your physical, mental, and emotional well-being. Some techniques that can help you build and sustain energy levels are the same as those highlighted in this book. These practices are effective, and I will continue to emphasise them.

Here are some of my top picks for boosting energy.

- **SLEEP!** Over emphasis, I know, but this HAS to be the number 1 energy source. Re-read Chapter 9 on sleep and start implementing it. Sleep must be your priority for healing and energy building.
- **Nutrition:** Crap in, crap out—simples!
- **Hydration:** Water, drink it, that is all.
- **Exercise:** Find the best one for you and do it.
- **Stress:** Deal with it; it's a chronic drain on your energy reserves.
- **Get organised:** set up systems, write lists, break down tasks, get a cleaner—do whatever it takes to reduce your load.
- **Stop overloading on sugar or caffeine:** you're on the energy rollercoaster; one minute, you're up, and the next, you've crashed. Reduce them both, and stick to the early morning caffeine.
- **Give yourself a break.** Get up from your desk, stretch, take a short walk, or engage in

activities that help clear your mind and renew your energy. Have a nap—I love a nap.

- **Spend time with people who make you happy.** Engage in social activities and cultivate positive relationships. Surround yourself with supportive and uplifting people who energise you. Remove the energy drainers (we all know who they are).
- **Incorporate meditation**, deep breathing exercises, or progressive muscle relaxation into your daily routine. Also, journal every day.
- **Minimise exposure to negative influences**, such as excessive screen time, toxic relationships, or environments that drain your energy. Identify and address factors that contribute to fatigue and adjust as necessary.
- **Dancing** or listening to loud music is one of my favourite vibration-lifting practices.
- **Get outside** in nature: I spend lots of time amongst the trees.

Remember that building and maintaining energy is gradual, and listening to your body's needs is essential. It's like your daily medicine.

Protecting your energy: Are you an elevator or a drain?

As you become more conscious of your energy levels, you'll recognise the people and circumstances that drain or uplift you. Pay attention to which situations or individuals fall into each category.

Naturally, avoiding everyone or everything that depletes your energy (such as ironing) is impossible. Still, you can reduce your exposure to the energy drainers and increase your exposure to the energy elevators. When you create awareness, it gives you choices.

I prioritise my energy and pay attention to my body's signals. I've learned to recognise when something is a definite "yes" or "no" for me. By embodying my core, my body communicates with me constantly, and I've become better at listening to these messages.

I've done this by being consistent with all the practices described in this book.

Chapter 15

The Chakra System

In discussing the subtle energies of the body, it is important to mention the chakra system. This concept originated from ancient Indian spiritual traditions, primarily within Hinduism, and has been adopted by other belief systems like Buddhism and New Age spirituality. The chakra system refers to a set of energy centres or wheels in the human body along the spine, each associated with different areas and aspects of life.

The term "chakra" comes from Sanskrit and means "wheel" or "disk." They are spinning energy centres that control the flow of vital life force, or prana, throughout the body. Each chakra connects to certain qualities, functions, and aspects of consciousness. There are many more chakras that are located on and around the body, but I'll focus on the main ones.

1. Root Chakra (Muladhara): At the base of the spine, it is associated with grounding, stability, survival, and physical well-being.
2. Sacral Chakra (Svadhishthana): In the lower abdomen, it is associated with creativity, sexuality, pleasure, and emotional balance.
3. Solar Plexus Chakra (Manipura): In the upper abdomen, it is associated with personal power, confidence, self-esteem, and willpower.
4. Heart Chakra (Anahata): In the centre of the chest, it is associated with love, compassion, forgiveness, and emotional healing.
5. Throat Chakra (Vishuddha): In the throat, it is associated with communication, self-expression, truth, and authenticity.
6. Third Eye Chakra (Ajna): Between the eyebrows, it is associated with intuition, insight, imagination, and spiritual awareness.
7. Crown Chakra (Sahasrara): At the top of the head, it is associated with spiritual connection, higher consciousness, divine wisdom, and enlightenment.

The chakras can significantly impact your physical, emotional, and spiritual well-being by interacting with each other. Balanced chakras with free energy flow contribute to overall health, harmony, and spiritual growth.

Each chakra links to organs, archetypes, planets, and colours, making it a magical system that has been around for centuries. When a chakra is out of balance, techniques like meditation, yoga, crystals, Breathwork, and energy healing are used to activate, cleanse, and balance them.

Everything is Vibration

"If you want to find the secrets of the universe, think in terms of energy, frequency and vibration."—Nikola Tesla

Quantum physics states that all things are in a state of vibration. This means particles and objects move back and forth in a specific motion. At the smallest level of matter, particles like electrons, protons, and neutrons have a wave-like nature with unique frequencies that determine their energy and properties.

The human body encompasses a wide range of vibrations, frequencies, and rhythms at different levels, so it's important to understand vibration.

The brain generates electrical activity we can measure with electroencephalography (EEG). It is classified into different frequency bands, such as delta (0.5-4 Hz), theta (4-8 Hz), alpha (8-12 Hz), beta (12-30 Hz), and gamma (above 30 Hz). Each frequency corresponds to different states of consciousness, such as deep sleep, relaxation, alertness, and focused attention. During meditation or Breathwork, the aim is to reach a gamma state, which requires lots of practice and involves increasing our vibration levels.

This is how sound healing or vocal toning (saying one

tone such as "Ohm" or humming) works. We're sending deep vibrations into our system to raise our vibration.

The Earth's atmosphere has a fascinating phenomenon known as Schumann resonances. These electromagnetic resonances happen between the Earth's surface and the ionosphere. The Schumann resonance's fundamental frequency is about 7.83 Hz and has harmonics at higher frequencies.

Did you know that every planet and moon has a unique vibration and frequency? By becoming more aware of your body and connecting on a cellular level, you can feel and sense the different frequencies that exist. Cultivating this awareness is important, as these frequencies are measurable and impact our overall well-being.

It is also believed that emotions have frequencies. Love and joy vibrate at a high frequency, while fear and shame vibrate at a low frequency. This concept is often related to the "vibrational frequency of emotions" or the "law of attraction." This suggests that similar frequencies attract or resonate with each other. By keeping positive emotions or high-frequency vibrations, we can attract positive experiences or outcomes into our lives.

Just as two violins in the same room will resonate at the same frequency when one is being played, humans also have a similar effect. When someone with a high vibration enters a room, you can feel a lift in the space, even though you may not know why.

Chapter 16

Archetypes—Your Unconscious Drivers

One thing I've found helpful in understanding what drives and influences us is the concept of archetypes. Swiss psychiatrist Carl Jung states archetypes are essential patterns and symbols in the collective unconscious. They are primordial images and ideas deeply rooted in human psychology and shared across cultures and societies.

Jung believed archetypes represent certain aspects of human experience and exist in the unconscious realm, influencing our thoughts, emotions, behaviours, and perceptions. These archetypes can take many forms, such as characters, themes, or motifs, and are often seen in myths, fairy tales, dreams, and religious symbolism.

Archetypes are recurring characters or themes we recognise in stories, movies, and cultural expressions. Some common archetypes include the hero, the mentor, the trickster, the wise old man/woman, the shadow, the mother, the father, and the child. These archetypes represent certain qualities that resonate with our experiences and aspirations. They help us understand the world and ourselves better. Archetypes are also valuable for personal development, as they provide rich symbolism and meaning to help navigate the complexities of human existence.

Here are a few common archetypes; see if you recognise them.

The Victim

The Victim archetype, first described by Carl Jung and studied by many psychologists and authors, refers to a pattern of behaviour and mindset where someone sees themselves as a victim of their circumstances, other people, or external forces. This archetype can show up in different forms and is based on the individual's feelings of powerlessness, helplessness, and being at the mercy of others.

Some common characteristics of the Victim archetype include:

Experiencing a sense of helplessness and believing you have little to no control over your life or circumstances.

Blaming external factors or other individuals for your misfortunes or challenges instead of taking responsibility for your choices and actions.

Seeking validation, sympathy, and support from others by emphasising your struggles. Hoping to receive attention and help.

Frequently engaging in self-pity, dwelling on your perceived unfairness of life and your negative experiences.

Victims may struggle to break free from their circumstances or patterns of behaviour as they may fear the unknown or lack the belief in their ability to change their situation.

Understand that the Victim archetype and other

archetypes are not fixed identities or permanent states. They are psychological patterns that can be identified, understood, and used for personal growth and empowerment. To overcome the Victim archetype, you must develop self-awareness, take responsibility for your choices and actions, build resilience, and regain personal power and control.

Do you notice any resonance with the Victim? Notice when they appear in your life and when you slip into Victim mode. Notice when the Victim shows up in others —how do you react?

The Saboteur (I meet a lot of these!)

The Saboteur archetype refers to a behavioural and mental pattern that involves self-sabotage, self-doubt, and a tendency to hinder one's success or well-being. This pattern can appear in different forms and is based on an individual's fears, insecurities, and negative self-perceptions.

Here are some characteristics often associated with the Saboteur archetype:

Acting in ways that hinder their progress, success, or happiness. This can include procrastinating, self-doubt, striving for perfection, or engaging in harmful habits.

The Saboteur archetype is often linked to the inner critic, an internal voice continuously criticising and undermining one's abilities, worth, or potential. This critical voice can reduce confidence and lead to a self-fulfilling prophecy of failure.

This archetype may be driven by a fear of success and the unknown changes it brings. The individual may worry about the responsibilities or expectations that come with success, leading them to undermine their efforts unconsciously.

Conversely, fear of failure can also be a driving force for the Saboteur archetype. The individual may engage in self-sabotaging behaviour to avoid the perceived pain or disappointment of failure.

The Saboteur archetype is often associated with negative self-beliefs and a tendency to focus on limitations, inadequacies, or past failures. These limiting beliefs can create a self-fulfilling cycle of negative outcomes.

When does your Saboteur show up? How can you stop yourself from sabotaging your success? When does the Saboteur show up in others?

"Would you like another glass of wine?"

"Oh, go on, it's just one piece of cake."

These are typical saboteur words!

The Wise Woman/Crone Archetype

This figure embodies someone with extensive knowledge, wisdom, and intuition. Typically portrayed as an older woman who has gained wisdom through life experiences, she deeply understands human nature. As we approach menopause, embracing her energy and power is essential. I channel this archetype the most (or I try to!).

The Wise Woman is known for her deep understanding of the world and the human psyche. A powerful woman who possesses knowledge of herbal remedies, spiritual practices, and ancient wisdom. She has a keen intuition and can perceive truths and insights not clear to others.

Her intuition guides her in making decisions and offering advice. She often has a healing role, both physically and emotionally. The Wise Woman is a mentor and guide, particularly to younger individuals or those seeking wisdom. She imparts her knowledge, teachings, and life lessons to help others on their paths.

The Wise Woman is often deeply connected to nature and the spiritual realm. She may revere the natural world, use natural elements in her healing practices, and offer spiritual guidance.

This archetype symbolises feminine wisdom and power, representing the collective knowledge and experience of generations of women. She is often portrayed as a source of strength, guidance, and inspiration, embodying the qualities of compassion, empathy, and understanding.

Can you see why I channel her often? When does the Wise Woman show up in your life? How can you embrace her more? What aspects of adopting the Wise Woman scare you?

How to Harness Your Archetypal Energy

It can be helpful to understand your archetypes, which ones you embody at any moment, and which ones appear in those around you. Are you attracting the same ones? This understanding can offer valuable insights into the patterns, beliefs, and behaviours that contribute to your pain. It brings awareness to the practices not serving you, so you can make conscious choices to address them; this is how I gave up alcohol.

Archetypes can shed light on the root causes of your pain. For example, the Victim archetype may reveal patterns of self-pity or a tendency to perceive yourself as powerless in the face of pain. The Saboteur archetype may expose self-sabotaging behaviours that worsen your pain. By understanding these underlying dynamics, you can address the root causes rather than solely focusing on the physical symptoms.

Archetypes offer alternative perspectives and narratives that can help you reframe your experience of pain. For instance, exploring the Warrior archetype can help you tap into your inner strength and resilience to face and overcome pain. The Wise Woman archetype may guide you in finding meaning or purpose within your pain. These shifts in perspective can help you develop a more empowering and constructive relationship with your pain.

Archetypes provide a language and symbolic framework to explore and express your emotions related to pain. By understanding the archetypal patterns at play, you can uncover suppressed emotions, unresolved traumas, or unmet needs which may contribute to your pain experience.

Start by journaling when your Victim and Saboteur show up in your life. See if you can think of any other Archetypes you embody: the Maiden (waiting to be rescued), the Warrior Woman (she's got a mission) and many more.

Grounding/Earthing

I'm a big fan of "Earthing" or "Grounding". Although it may seem on the hippy side, considering how far we've evolved from our natural state as humans, we rarely connect directly with our planet in the modern world. We are constantly surrounded by and in contact with devices that interfere with our natural frequencies: there is Wi-Fi in our homes and 5G in our atmosphere. We're surrounded by frequencies that never existed 25 years ago.

I walk barefoot as much as possible and touch trees (yes, I'm a tree hugger too). Not only does it make me feel good—I'm all for calming down my nervous system—but there is some science behind it too.

Earthing, also known as grounding, involves:

Physically connecting with the Earth's surface in various ways, such as walking barefoot.

Standing on grass, soil, or sand.

Using conductive systems that allow direct contact with the Earth (I sleep on an Earthing sheet).

Earthing involves absorbing the Earth's natural electrical energy, which can help balance and restore the body's electrical state. It is based on the idea that the Earth has a negative electrical charge, and when we touch the Earth, our bodies receive electrons that counteract excess positive charges. The practice is believed to have many health benefits, particularly in reducing chronic inflammation associated with various health issues. By promoting a more balanced immune response, grounding can help decrease inflammation.

Studies have shown that grounding, or connecting with the Earth's electrical energy, can improve the quality and length of sleep. It helps regulate the body's circadian rhythms and melatonin production, which is crucial for maintaining healthy sleep patterns.

It's worth a try!

Chapter 17

Boundaries

To become fully embodied, it's important to have boundaries. Boundaries mean setting and maintaining limits for yourself in relationships, interactions, and different aspects of life. They are crucial for establishing and maintaining personal autonomy, self-care, and healthy relationships. They help you define what behaviour you will and will not accept from others and from yourself.

This is where practising your "Sacred Yes" and "Sacred No" come in.

Emotional boundaries involve recognising and respecting your emotions and the emotions of others. It includes understanding and communicating personal feelings, needs, and limits, while also respecting the emotions and boundaries of others.

Physical boundaries involve personal space, touch, and physical interactions. It entails limiting how close others can get physically and defining what kind of touch or physical contact is comfortable and appropriate.

Time boundaries relate to managing and allocating your time and energy. It involves setting aside time for self-care, personal interests, work, relationships, and other commitments. Establishing boundaries around time helps prevent over-commitment and burnout.

Social boundaries involve determining the level of interaction and involvement in social situations. It includes deciding which relationships to engage in, which social environments to take part in, and the level of privacy or disclosure of personal information you're comfortable with.

Material boundaries pertain to personal possessions, resources, and finances. It involves setting limits on how others share, borrow, or use your belongings or resources and establishing financial boundaries to protect your financial well-being.

Having healthy boundaries means:

- Knowing and communicating your needs, desires, and limits.
- Being able to say "no" without feeling guilty. The "Sacred No."
- Respecting and valuing your well-being, emotions, and values.
- Respecting and valuing the well-being, feelings, and values of others.
- Maintaining a balance between giving and receiving in relationships.
- Recognising and addressing situations where boundaries are being violated or disrespected.

Establishing and maintaining boundaries is an ongoing process that requires self-awareness, self-assertiveness, and effective communication. Once you have your boundaries in place and stick to them, you will respect yourself and others much more. Just watch how boundaries change you and your world.

In your journal, write some of your boundaries down.

Chapter 18

Polyvagal Theory

Dr Stephen Porges developed Polyvagal Theory in the 1990s. It's a theory of how our nervous system affects our behaviour, emotions, and social interactions. It's worthy of a mention here, as it connects quite a few of the concepts we've already met in this book.

The vagus nerve, also known as the tenth cranial nerve X, is a long-paired nerve that originates in the brainstem and branches out to multiple body areas. The vagus nerve has sensory and motor functions, innervating multiple organs and tissues in the body. It branches to various structures in the head and neck region, including the throat, larynx (voice box), tongue, and sensory areas of the ear. It extends into the thoracic, abdominal, and pelvic cavities. The vagus nerve used to be called the "wandering nerve" as that's what it seemed to do all over the body.

The vagus nerve calms the stress responses in the heart, lungs, digestive system, stomach, liver, spleen, pancreas, intestines, and reproductive organs. This nerve significantly influences heart rate, controls bronchial smooth muscle, and regulates digestive functions. Remember the Gut-Brain axis? This is the how they talk to each other.

According to Polyvagal Theory, the Autonomic Nervous System consists of three interconnected branches:

1. Ventral Vagal Complex (VVC): This branch promotes social engagement and connection. When the VVC is active, it supports feelings of safety, calmness, and connection with others.
2. Sympathetic Nervous System (SNS): The SNS is associated with the "fight-or-flight" response. The vagus nerve prepares the body for action in response to a perceived threat or stressor. It activates when the VVC does not detect safety, leading to increased heart rate, blood pressure, and other physiological responses associated with stress and mobilisation.
3. Dorsal Vagal Complex (DVC): The DVC referred to as the "freeze" response. When activated, it promotes immobilisation, dissociation, and shutdown as a response to extreme danger or overwhelming stress.

According to the theory, people with a well-regulated vagus nerve can easily connect with others, feel secure, and handle stress effectively. Conversely, those with an irregular vagus nerve may have problems with social interaction, struggle with managing their emotions, and be more vulnerable to stress-related illnesses.

To regulate the autonomic nervous system and promote a sense of security and well-being, here are some exercises inspired by the Polyvagal Theory.

- Deep Belly Breathing: Place one hand on your belly and take slow, deep breaths, allowing your stomach to rise and fall with each breath. Focus on extending the exhale to activate the VVC and promote relaxation.
- Self-Soothing Touch: Engage in gentle self-soothing touch by stroking your arms, hands, or face with care and warmth.
- Progressive Muscle Relaxation: Starting from your toes, systematically tense and then release each muscle group.
- Grounding Techniques: Engage your senses to ground yourself in the present moment.
- Notice five things you can see, four things you can touch, three things you can hear, two things you can smell, and one thing you can taste.
- Vocal Toning: Make soothing sounds or hum gently to activate the VVC and stimulate the vagus nerve. Experiment with different vocal tones and pitches to find what feels relaxing and calming.
- Safe and Calm Visualisation: Close your eyes and imagine yourself in a safe, peaceful, and calming environment. Visualise the details of this place, such as the sights, sounds, and sensations.

It's worth further reading if you're interested in learning more.

Chapter 19

What Does it Mean to Live a Spiritual Life?

Having boundaries and a vision

"Spiritual health is the most important of the four bodies and the driver of physical health."—Jill

I love incense sticks, crystals, and a floaty dress as much as the next person, but that's not what living a spiritual life is all about.

"We sacrifice our health to make wealth; then we sacrifice our wealth to regain our health."—Dalai Lama

Becoming fully embodied is having a vision, planning, and then acting upon it. Trust that the universe has your back. You are the co-creator of your life; you are more in control than you think. Practising spiritual health is about taking responsibility for your choices and actions.

I know what it feels like to be stuck in a corporate job; how you feel trapped, and you know your health is suffering. There is another way; you must reconnect to that vision. I connected to my dream and took positive action; a series of coincidences helped me on the way (or were they?) It was scary to take that leap into self-employment, knowing it was down to me to make money. It was also the most empowering thing I've ever down, and it took me on a magical, mystical tour of growth and expansion.

When you live a spiritual way, you understand that we have a choice to be happy at every moment. Happiness is an inside job. Since I stopped drinking alcohol, I get high on life; I notice the small things I've never done before.

I am sovereign of my body. My body is my temple; it's the only place I must live so I will look after it—just like the planet. I understand that my energetic body is as important as my physical body; I don't let anyone step into my energy field who doesn't respect this (hello, boundaries). Your spiritual health depends on your physical health.

Most "spiritual" people I know are waist-deep in sorting their s**t out, not dancing naked around stone circles (although, yes, we are a bit partial to that too). Knowing that to progress and evolve in life, we must let go of ego and what other people think and let go of self-limiting beliefs. We spend a lot of time on our own; indeed, in indigenous cultures, if you felt out of balance or depressed, the shaman would ask you three questions.

- When did you stop dancing?
- When did you stop singing?
- When did you stop enjoying your own sweet company?

Being "spiritual" means spending a lot of time sitting with your feelings, not blocking them out—and reflecting on your triggers. It does not mean we don't have issues or annoyances; it means we don't let those issues get in the way of living our best lives.

When you're on a spiritual path, you understand

everything is happening for us, not to us. Everything is a lesson or a blessing, and that's how we expand. We build lives we don't need holidays from. From the outside, it looks like we're living full and carefree lives, but that requires much work and determination. Knowing your worth, values, and boundaries is vital, and sticking to them!

It also requires giving up things we think we need, like corporate jobs that kill us, alcohol that's poison, and processed foods that are crap. The things we need are the things holding us back. When you look deeply at your life, you'll make stunning transformations and bring conscious awareness.

Are you ready to become more aware of the choices you're making?

Conclusion

And take a deep breath. There's a lot to take in, but once you start to drop into your own intuition, trust you will know where to start. Bring awareness to your life: what are you not changing? What are you choosing?

I hope I've given you enough food for thought and perhaps a different perspective on your pain and lifestyle. And that you're ready to get started on your healthy lifestyle and healing journey to becoming fully embodied with your core. It's a lifelong journey, but once you step down into the rabbit hole, you'll find it's a magical, wondrous journey into your soul.

There will be joy and there will be setbacks, and you'll find that some weeks you feel amazing, and others you'll feel like you've jumped back six weeks. Just know this is all part of the journey and it's never a linear process. If you stick to the healthy lifestyle options as much as you can, you will start to make some positive changes.

This book should be used as your guide but remember to do your own research. You need to take control of your condition and start taking an active role in your recovery. I hope I've given you enough avenues to explore to get your health and your mindset in the right place.

Little and often is the key.

Good luck with making your changes—you deserve to live a pain free life.

Movement is medicine. Day one, or one day—you decide. Let your deep bodily wisdom guide you, and trust the process.

Big Love,

Jill x

Appendix 1: Baseline Questions

Right here, right now—let's take some baseline measurements. You can write these here, or in your journal.

- What is your top priority in your health right now, and why?
- If you did nothing, where do you see yourself in 5 years?
- What small steps can you begin to introduce right now?
- What will be your challenges in being consistent?
- What can you put in place to remain on track?
- How will you hold yourself accountable, or who can you ask to hold you accountable?
- How will you know you're making progress?
- In 6 months what changes would you like to see?
- How will you reward yourself when you reach a milestone?

Appendix 2: Monthly Accountability Sheet

Use this wheel of your life to see where you are, repeat each month.

Month:

Are you happy with your balance?

Appendix 2: Monthly Accountability Sheet

Yes – how will I maintain it?

No – how will I improve it?

What went right last month?

Achievements

Appendix 3: Physical Check-In

Month:

Calculate Your Waist to Hip Ratio

- Get a measuring tape
- Measure your waist and hips
- Divide your waist measurement by your hip measurement

A waist to hip ratio of more than 0.95 for men and 0.85 for women is 'apple' shape - more prone to heart disease.

0.90+	Extreme
0.85 - 0.90	High
0.80 - 0.85	Average
0.75 - 0.80	Good
<0.75	Excellent

WAIST/HIP RATIO	
	MEASUREMENTS
CHEST	
WAIST	
BELLY BUTTON	
HIPS	
R THIGH	
R BICEP	

Changes from last month?

Am I where I want to be?

Appendix 4: Protein Smoothie Ideas

Smoothies are a great way to up your daily protein. Here are some recipes for you to try.

Berry Blast:

- 1 cup mixed berries (strawberries, blueberries, raspberries)
- 1 banana
- 1 scoop of your favourite protein powder (such as whey, pea, or soy protein)
- 1 cup almond milk (or any milk of your choice)

Optional: 1 tbsp almond butter or chia seeds for added nutrition

Green Powerhouse:

- 2 cups spinach or kale
- 1 ripe pear
- 1/2 cucumber

- 1/2 avocado
- 1 scoop of plant-based protein powder (such as hemp, rice, or pea protein)
- 1 cup coconut water (or regular water)

Optional: Fresh mint or a squeeze of lemon for extra freshness

Tropical Paradise:

- 1 cup frozen mango chunks
- 1/2 cup pineapple chunks
- 1 small ripe banana
- 1 scoop of vanilla protein powder
- 1 cup coconut milk (or any milk of your choice)

Optional: A handful of spinach for added nutrients

Chocolate Peanut Butter Delight:

- 1 cup unsweetened almond milk (or any milk of your choice)
- 1 scoop of chocolate protein powder
- 1 tablespoon natural peanut butter
- 1 small ripe banana

Optional: A handful of ice cubes for thickness and chill factor

Coffee Lover's Boost:

- 1 cup cold brewed coffee (or 1 shot of espresso)
- 1 scoop of vanilla or mocha-flavoured protein powder

- 1 tablespoon almond butter or cashew butter
- 1 ripe banana
- 1 cup almond milk (or any milk of your choice)

Optional: A sprinkle of cinnamon or a dash of vanilla extract for extra flavour

Feel free to adjust the quantities and ingredients according to your taste preferences and dietary needs. You can also add ice cubes to any of these recipes if you prefer a colder smoothie.

Enjoy your protein-packed smoothie!

Appendix 5: 30 Different Plants to Include in Your Weekly Diet

How many of these can you fit into your diet each week?

You can also include coffee (it's from a bean!) and chocolate (Cacao)—obviously the rawest form and highest qualities are best, not coffee from a jar or highly processed chocolate.

Use this list as a check sheet, and also write your own on too—I think you'll be surprised how many you can fit in especially if you include spices and make a lot of curries or stews!

- Spinach
- Broccoli
- Kale
- Avocado
- Blueberries
- Strawberries
- Raspberries
- Tomatoes
- Bell peppers
- Carrots

- Sweet potatoes
- Brussels sprouts
- Cauliflower
- Asparagus
- Green beans
- Quinoa
- Brown rice
- Lentils
- Chickpeas
- Black beans
- Almonds
- Walnuts
- Chia seeds
- Flaxseeds
- Pumpkin seeds
- Oats
- Whole wheat bread
- Tofu
- Edamame
- Coconut milk (as a dairy alternative)

This list includes a diverse range of plant foods that offer various essential nutrients, including vitamins, minerals, fibre, healthy fats, and plant-based proteins.

Appendix 6: How to Massage Your Stomach

Doing a stomach massage may help you go to the toilet. Massaging your stomach can help stimulate digestion and help relieve constipation. Here's a simple technique you can try:

- Find a comfortable position: lie down on your back or sit up in a relaxed position.
- Apply gentle pressure: place your fingertips or palm on your abdomen, just below the navel.
- Start with clockwise circular motions: using gentle and slow clockwise circular motions, begin massaging your abdomen. Gradually increase the pressure as tolerated but be careful not to apply too much force or discomfort.
- Expand the massage area: slowly expand the circular motions outward, covering a larger area of your abdomen. Continue the clockwise motion.
- Focus on specific areas: pay attention to any areas that feel particularly tight or tender. You

can spend more time massaging those areas using small circular motions or gentle kneading.

- Deep breathing: while massaging, take slow, deep breaths. This can help relax your abdominal muscles and enhance the massage's effectiveness.
- Continue for a few minutes: massage your abdomen for about 5-10 minutes, or longer if it feels comfortable.

You can repeat this several times throughout the day or whenever you feel the need for relief.

It's important to note that while abdominal massage can provide relief for some individuals, it may not be suitable for everyone, particularly those with certain medical conditions or abdominal sensitivities. If you have any concerns or chronic digestive issues, consult with a healthcare professional for guidance and to rule out any underlying causes of constipation.

Appendix 7: Journal Prompts

This is where the juicy stuff lies; if you want to get to the root of your pain and start to build towards a better future, then you're going to have to "get comfortable being uncomfortable" (as Wim Hof would say). Answering some of these questions may be challenging; you may not want to do it, and you might need more time to prepare for what they bring to the surface.

I say feel your way into them; that's not a "get off the hook" but do the questions you can answer quickly; look at the ones you're avoiding—you might find some gold in that alone. Why are you avoiding those questions?

I think you know already… am I right?

Find space and time; you don't have to spend hours pondering them. Try to switch off your thinking brain; just let your hand free write. See what comes up. When you first try free writing, nonsense might come up; that's fine. Keep going, and you never know what's going to appear.

> *"Until you make the unconscious conscious, it will direct your life. And you will call it fate."*—Carl Jung

Baseline

These are the questions I would like you to journal at the beginning of your journey.

1. Where in my body do I feel pain the most right now? (Remember to date it)
2. How do I rate my pain on a scale of 1-10 (1 being not an all, 10 being the most painful ever)?
3. What am I doing to help ease my pain? (Include medications)
4. What eases my pain?
5. What makes it worse?
6. On a scale of 1-10 (1 being not at all, 10 being wholly committed), how much are you willing to make some changes to improve your pain?

Ok, right there, you'll have a few answers. Start planning, and let's see if we can go deeper.

These are journal prompts; you can use mine or make your own. Regular journaling will help you to improve your pain or at least give you an idea of how far you've gone. We often forget when the pain has gone, just how bad it was. If you feel your motivation slipping, revisiting your answers will firmly put your healthy lifestyle habits back in their place.

Use these prompts to help you.

1. What excites me right now?
2. What would I love to learn?
3. Where in my life do I invite play?
4. What beliefs and fears are holding me back? How do I upgrade them?

5. What would I do right now if I was confident in my body?
6. What would it mean to be pain-free?
7. What do I want more of in my life?
8. What have I done well this week? How can I improve or build on this for next week?
9. What triggers my pain, and why?
10. What does my heart truly desire?
11. What would that look like if I were to improve by just 1%? How would that make me feel?
12. Where am I sabotaging myself?
13. What do you wish others understood about you?
14. What do I need to hear right now?
15. If I knew I couldn't fail, I would…
16. What did I learn from my family about money?
17. How do I feel about money? How do I want to feel about money?
18. What does feeling embodied mean to me?
19. What am I passionate about?
20. What does my "true self" have to say today?
21. Where am I adjusting to other people's opinions?
22. What am I ready for?
23. What am I ready to receive?
24. What am I avoiding right now?
25. What's my favourite thing about me? What's my favourite thing about my body?
26. What are my boundaries around my health?
27. What is my purpose in life?
28. When does my "people pleaser" personality show up?
29. When I'm feeling my best, I'm doing…

Those should keep you busy for a while. Don't be afraid to go deep.

Mulder and Scully were wrong: the truth isn't out there; it's in here!

Here's some further reading for you to continue your journey:

- *Explain Pain*—David Butler and Lorimer Moseley
- *Biology of Belief*—Dr Bruce Lipton
- *How to Eat, Move and Be Healthy*—Paul Chek

Further Reading

Here's some further reading if you're interested in the research documents.

Pain & Research on Women and Back Pain

https://pubmed.ncbi.nlm.nih.gov/18287824/

https://www.ncbi.nlm.nih.gov/pmc/articles/PMC3688274/

https://www.ncbi.nlm.nih.gov/pmc/articles/PMC6994312/

https://www.sciencedirect.com/science/article/pii/S0004951406700575?via%3Dihub

Stress

https://www.cell.com/cell-reports-medicine/pdfExtended/S2666-3791(22)00474-8

https://www.ncbi.nlm.nih.gov/pmc/articles/PMC5546756/

Bowel Health

https://pubmed.ncbi.nlm.nih.gov/18287824/

QR Code

Point your phone or iPad camera here and it'll take you to the sign-up page. Once you've entered your details, you'll receive your 6-Week Plan Videos and more.

About the Author

Find me online:
www.organicpilates.co.uk—where you can sign up to my weekly newsletter.
Podcast: *The Super-Natural Podcast* hosted by Podbean, available on Spotify, iTunes, Audible etc.

facebook.com/OrganicPilatesandHolisticHealth
instagram.com/organic_pilates_and_breathwork

Printed in Great Britain
by Amazon

33407104R00090